A Captive
Voice

A Captive
Voice

The Liberation
of Preaching

DAVID BUTTRICK

WESTMINSTER/JOHN KNOX PRESS
LOUISVILLE, KENTUCKY

Book and cover design by Drew Stevens

First edition

Published by Westminster/John Knox Press
Louisville, Kentucky

This book is printed on acid-free paper that meets the American National Standards Institute Z39.48 standard. ∞

PRINTED IN THE UNITED STATES OF AMERICA

9 8 7 6 5 4 3 2 1

Library of Congress Cataloging-in-Publication Data

Buttrick, David, date.
    A captive voice : the liberation of preaching / David Buttrick. —
1st ed.
        p.   cm.
    Includes bibliographical references and index.
    ISBN 0-664-25540-X (alk. paper)
    1. Preaching.   I. Title.
BV4211.2.B858   1994
251—dc20   93-31034

For Anne

Contents

Preface

In 1992 I was honored by an invitation to inaugurate the Donald Macleod Lectures at Princeton Theological Seminary. The first three chapters of this book are based on the Macleod Lectures.

A Canadian by birth, Dr. Donald Macleod joined the Princeton faculty in 1947, where he taught for thirty-six years. He was named the Francis Landey Patton Professor of Preaching and Worship. Dr. Macleod published eleven books, as well as many articles. He was instrumental in the founding of a scholarly society, the Academy of Homiletics. Dr. Macleod was a preacher, teacher, writer, and editor. And he still is—a vigorous Donald Macleod was present at the lectures.

The lectureship was a gift from the Short Hills Community Congregational Church in Short Hills, New Jersey. The Pastor of the church, Dr. Kenyon J. Wildrick, is a graduate of Princeton Theological Seminary. Dr. and Mrs. Wildrick, as well as other ministers of the Short Hills church, Dr. Virginia L. Scott and the Rev. Johann J. Bosman, attended the lectureship.

I am grateful for the welcome I received at Princeton Seminary. President and Mrs. Thomas Gillespie were gracious in their hospitality. Dean Conrad H. Massa and members of the faculty were most cordial. As always, I enjoyed being with Professor Thomas G. Long, a splendid homiletician. He and his wife Sherrill were most kind, and I am grateful for their friendship.

Chapter 4 of this book is drawn from a lecture given at A Festival of Preaching, sponsored by the Church of England's College of Preachers and held at the College of Ripon and York St. John in York, England. I am especially grateful to the Rev. Eric Young, Warden of the College of Preachers, and to the Rev. Arthur H. R. Quinn, who directed the festival. I also recall with appreciation the Rt. Rev. Michael Turnbull, the Bishop of Rochester, and chairman of the College of Preachers, who introduced me with wit and generosity. Lord Coggin, previously Archbishop of Canterbury, spoke eloquently of preaching as an offering. He, along with Lady Coggin, gave gracious presence to the event. I also am grateful to Canon Peter Southwell-Sander, who was a splendid guide and whom I count a friend.

I have added an Afterword to the chapters, a portion of which was delivered at A Festival of Homiletics in Williamsburg, Virginia, sponsored by the journal *Lectionary Homiletics*. The event was under the direction of the editor, the Rev. David B. Howell. I was welcomed by the Rev. Jan Rivero and, later, introduced by the Rev. Richard L. May.

These chapters are an attempt to reconsider the nature of preaching. We have only recently emerged from the biblical theology movement. We look now toward a future that will be ordered by a new and very different Christian consciousness—the consciousness of oppressed peoples emerging within Western culture and of those we tend to label, denigratingly, as third- or fourth-world. Thus these essays are at best transitional.

I owe a debt of appreciation to Dean Joseph C. Hough, Jr., of The Divinity School at Vanderbilt University for his sensitive support. And my faculty colleagues have taught me more than I can possibly acknowledge.

I am also indebted to two good homileticians. The Rev. Robert Howard chased down references and prepared many of the notes. The Rev. David Jacobsen helpfully straightened out my indexing. They are both unusually gifted and soon should be fine professors in the field.

As always, I am more than grateful to Betty More Allaben Buttrick. How do you say to someone you live with, and dearly love, that you do love her, that you would not write books without her presence in your life, that she is filled with delight, prompts free laughter, and gives sweet gifts wherever she goes? My goodness, I seem to have done so.

Mostly I write for ministers and for ministerial students. I enjoy them. And I do hope the book may be helpful.

D.G.B.

The Divinity School
Vanderbilt University

Acknowledgments

Grateful acknowledgment is made to the following for permission to reprint copyrighted materials.

Grove/Atlantic, Inc. for excerpt from the book *Exit the King, and Other Plays*, by Eugene Ionesco, Copyright © 1960 by John Calder. Used with permission.

Harcourt Brace & Company, and Faber & Faber, for excerpt from "Choruses from 'The Rock,'" in *Collected Poems 1909–1962*, by T. S. Eliot, copyright 1936 by Harcourt Brace & Company, copyright © 1964, 1965 by T. S. Eliot, reprinted by permission of the publisher.

Alfred A. Knopf, Inc., for quotation from *Collected Poems* by Wallace Stevens, Copyright 1936 by Wallace Stevens and renewed 1964 by Holly Stevens. Reprinted by permission.

Introduction

The scheme of the book is simple.

We will be looking at some good things—Bible, church, and Christian identity in the world—good things that may have turned against us.

The recovery of the Bible in the twentieth century was, all in all, a good thing. Surely, the church should recall identity in every age by recovering sources. If the church, like an amnesiac, has forgotten the scriptural story, then the church cannot grasp who and why it is in God's purposes. So, during the century, once more we turned to the scriptures seeking to find ourselves in faith. Karl Barth's *The Epistle to the Romans*, published in 1919, seemed to inaugurate a neo-orthodox return to sources. With a vivid image, Barth likened himself to a man climbing a bell tower who, to steady himself, grabbed a rope by mistake, thus tolling a bell for everyone to hear. Perhaps Barth's early work did reverberate, calling us back to scripture.

But somehow Barth's Word of God theology may have turned against us. In America, the political right wing appears to have taken over the Bible. Does not the Rev. Pat Robertson use the Bible to endorse a hawkish America and at the same time to put down the rights of women, castigate members of the gay/lesbian community, support subtle forms of resurgent

1

racism, and accuse those who argue "pro-choice" of being murderers? A frightened cultural status quo seems to have pasted its own labels on the Bible. Meanwhile, the mainline pulpits are politely silent, perhaps because they too are busy preaching the scriptures. The Bible is surely a good gift of God, a light and a delight. But has the Bible, a wondrous gift, suddenly turned against preaching?

Again, in mid-twentieth century, we saw a renewal of ecclesiology. The new ecclesiology was liberating. We began to realize that the church's ministry is corporate; by baptism, all church members have been ordained to a common ministry. As a part of the push for a broader, more egalitarian church, preaching seems to have undergone reconception. The high-hung pulpits from which Reformers thundered were scaled down to size. Preaching is, after all, a kind of conversation at table, a helpful word among friends in Christ. In many ways, the change was right and good. Disciplined liturgy returned to the barren meetinghouses of our American Protestant heritage. We began to speak of Word and Sacrament as normative. As for preaching, well, was it not time for some pulpit modesty? We turned off the spotlights that used to circle our pulpits in darkened church naves and began to speak as "one without authority." After all, were we not all ministers in a common ministry? Surely preaching must change and become the articulation of our common faith, a speaking from the Spirit we all possess. Let preaching be *our* word! The result has been a tempering of the pulpit. We preach to articulate the faith of community, or we preach to enable the church in mission. But the notion that preaching is somehow the voice of God—well, such a supposition has all but faded away. So are we left to live comforting one another therapeutically in the absence of God?

What about culture? In an earlier age, toward the start of the century, there was genuine apologetic desire to converse with the culture. Has not the church in every age been concerned to quicken human awareness of God. Often, awareness of God is not much more than "restlessness" (Augustine), or "anxiety" (Reinhold Niebuhr), or a once-in-a-while flicker of "ultimate concern" (Paul Tillich). Maybe, in our secular world, awareness of God can be nothing more than a name, or a vague, leftover memory of forgotten ritual, as in some Woody Allen film. But in earlier times, the church was out in the world trying to make a case for God. We preachers were evangelistic, and we were apologetic, and sometimes we were even boldly critical of cultural notions. We were engaged with the world. But then, with the rise of dialectical theology, the pulpit stopped conversing with the world, particularly a secular world, which we tended to regard as a potentially corrupting enemy. Instead, we gripped our Bibles tightly. After all, they were filled with God's Word, a word that was certainly not available anywhere else. The result has been peculiar. We gave up naming God in the world and instead tried to urge the world to please come into our churches where the Bibles were. Somehow in our zeal for an uncorrupted biblical faith, we lost touch with worldly neighbors, and, in losing touch, left the world—a world God loves—to "other gods." Has the smart apologetic fire of the pulpit turned into burnout?

In chapter 4, we will look at method, the problem of how to preach. Nineteenth-century homiletics drew on rhetorical study. In the twentieth century, homiletic wisdom was reduced, while at the same time the connection between homiletics and rhetoric was severed. We decided to preach the Bible, to draw method from the Bible, and to turn away from the machinations of secular rhetoric. The result: We made biblical noises but in fact we did not preach very well. Of course, the black pulpit continued to speak with force, the force of a highly sophisticated black rhetorical tradition. But note, as theology moves toward philosophy and as biblical criticism connects with literary criticism, homiletics must shyly make up and relate to rhetoric once again.

So the chapters to follow will challenge preaching. Perhaps you will discover that, though the pages may seem contentious, they will not be unthoughtful. Nor will they be without a deep undercurrent of evangelical passion. If we are critical of current pulpit practices, we will be trying to find some new way to speak. In the Afterword, we will look into the tomorrow of preaching. The renewal of the pulpit is, after all, a theological task. Catholic or Protestant, ordained or unordained, we are all called by God to speak, and therefore we must all become theologians of the Word.

3

1

Preaching and Bible

Have you noticed? When American preachers preach, they usually have an open Bible on hand. Most often they have an enormous pulpit Bible, opened to the Psalms so that the book is level. Sometimes, for revivals, there's a limp, one-hand-held Bible. And a few months ago on Sunday-morning television, a preacher preached in front of a backdrop Bible that filled the entire stage. Obviously, most American Protestants associate preaching with the Bible. But, here's a question: Must preaching be from the Bible? Could the stage backdrop be something else—a picture of Christ or a church steeple or perhaps the faces of an average congregation? Exactly what is the relationship between Bible and preaching?

The Rise and Fall of Biblical Theology

Let us begin by locating ourselves. We are children, all of us, of a twentieth-century biblical theology movement.[1] The biblical theology movement began to emerge early in the century at about the same time as did self-conscious fundamentalism.[2] The movement has been astonishingly productive.

Commentaries have multiplied; the ICC, the IB, the AB, the NIC, all the way to *Interpretation, Hermeneia,* and beyond.[3] Now, like *Terminator* movies, we're getting IB2 and ICC2; should we expect a Son of Hermeneia soon? During the century, Bible study materials have been hustled off religious presses, wave after wave, everything from the Presbyterian Church's remarkable Faith and Life Curriculum in the 1940s and 1950s to the currently popular *Kerygma* series, all geared to further biblical literacy in local congregations. In theological seminaries, students laughingly sang the jingle, "The B-I-B-L-E / yes, that's the book for me!" Though students laughed, the jingle was actually a confession of faith. Most American Christians at the end of the twentieth century had been taught by a once-dominant biblical theology movement.[4]

In homiletics, the movement had a similar impact. Back in 1907, P. T. Forsyth's Yale Lectures urged a return to biblical faith and, above all, to biblical preaching.[5] Then in 1928 came the English translation of Karl Barth's *The Word of God and the Word of Man*—so full of passion, faith, and exclamation points! Barth argued somewhat optimistically that congregations come to church with

> . . . a passionate longing to lay hold of *that* which, or rather of *him* who, overcomes the world because he is its Creator and Redeemer, its beginning and ending and Lord, a passionate longing to have the *word* spoken, *the* word which promises grace in *judgment,* life in *death,* and the beyond in the *here and now, God's* word—this it is which animates our church-goers, however lazy, bourgeois, or commonplace may be the manner in which they express their want in so-called real life.[6]

But where, according to Barth, is the italicized *word* to be found? He goes on to affirm the Bible as Word of God.

> If the congregation brings to church the great *question* of human life and *seeks* an *answer* for it, the Bible contrariwise brings an *answer,* and *seeks* the *question* corresponding to this answer; it seeks questioning *people* who are eager to find and

able to understand that its seeking of them is the very answer to their question.[7]

Barth personified scripture; the Bible was God's own passionate voice, bespeaking a saving concern for humanity. Later he devoted more than three hundred pages of *Church Dogmatics* to explicating the notion that "Scripture is recognized as the Word of God by the fact that it *is* the Word of God"—a truth that could only be confessed by the church.[8]

Barth was influential. Donald Miller, prompted by both Forsyth and Barth, wrote two useful books in the 1950s on the how-to's of what he termed "biblical preaching."[9] Then a brace of Barthian thinkers, Dietrich Ritschl and Jean-Jacques von Allmen, penned theologies of proclamation, tying a tight knot between Bible and pulpit.[10] And in the 1970s and early 1980s there appeared a delayed rash of "text-to-sermon" books, by Reginald Fuller, Leander Keck, and Ernest Best, among others.[11]

Then, to top off the triumphs of biblical theology, a second wave of liturgical renewal[12] swept us into lectionary preaching. With a shared lectionary, groups of clergy began to meet in American villages and together prepared sermons from scripture. Even today, the movement has not abated; the journal *Lectionary Preaching* has a whopping subscription list, and exegetical/homiletic aids, such as the Proclamation series, are designed according to common lectionary readings. More and more preachers are relying on lectionary guides in the preparation of sermons. Has any era had more biblical preaching than our own age? For most of the century, Protestant pulpits have been governed by an ascendant biblical theology movement.

Of course, the biblical theology movement was more than a concern for biblical literacy; it was a theology as well. The biblical theology movement rode the crest of neo-orthodoxy and surely found its flowering in the work of Karl Barth.[13] His "dialectical theology" was set over against turn-of-the-century theological liberalism. Barth denied general revelation in both nature and religious experience; nature was ceded to the scientists; and Friedrich Schleiermacher, who had argued from human experience, was viewed with suspicion.[14] Instead, biblical theology insisted that revelation was in history, through "mighty acts of God"[15] and, singularly, in the history of God-with-us, Jesus Christ of Nazareth. In Barth you can trace a kind of biblical authority by descent: God is God, transcendent and unknowable, but God is self-revealed in the Word of God, namely Jesus Christ, and Jesus Christ is written down in a witness to the Word of God, namely the Bible, and the Bible is in turn what preachers preach to the faithful so that their sermons also may be labeled Word of God.

Barth wrote more about preaching than any theologian in history; indeed, he regarded his *Church Dogmatics* as a theology for preachers.[16] Nevertheless, Barth in some ways all but destroyed preaching in the name of the Bible. He threw out sermon introductions because they might imply some sort of "point of contact," some natural affinity for the gospel in the human sphere;[17] and he lopped off conclusions because they might express works-righteousness.[18] Above all, he denied social relevance: "The Preacher," he wrote, "must preach the Bible and *nothing* else."[19] As a result, preaching became for Barth the reiteration of a biblical text—"like the involuntary lip movement of one who is reading" scripture[20]—without much reference to the social world. Though Barth is associated with the brave Barmen Declaration, his homiletic writings from the same period already seem to be moving him toward a kind of biblical isolation in which public events are excised from sermons.[21]

> The application or reference does not always have to be *à jour*. We do not always have to bring in the latest and most sensational events. For instance, if a fire broke out in the community last week, and church members are still suffering under its awful impact, we should be on guard against even hinting at this theme in the sermon. It belongs to everyday life, but now it is Sunday, and people do not want to remain stuck in everyday problems.[22]

For a decade that included World War I, Barth was a parish preacher, yet he regretted ever having mentioned the war in his sermons.[23] Preaching, he argued, must aim "beyond the hill of relevance."[24]

Karl Barth's achievement is truly awesome; he wrote book after book. Though unfinished at the time of his death, his *Church Dogmatics*, including two brief, posthumously published volumes, rambled through more than eighty-seven hundred pages, an intellectual achievement beyond the scope of most mortal minds. As a result, many contemporary Protestants have all but conferred sainthood on Karl Barth, without recourse to a Devil's Advocate. With Barth in the vanguard, the biblical theology movement triumphed in most American Protestant pulpits.

So Much for Prophecy!

Now stop and add up results. For the better part of the twentieth century, preaching and Bible have been wrapped up in a kind of incestuous relationship. What has been the issue? What has been the result of biblical theology in our churches? At the outset, underscore *a strange silence on public affairs*.[25] Though Barthians joined the protest movements of the 1960s—God's Word was *always* countercultural—such involvement was short-lived; it seemed to end with the decade. In America of late, with the social right wing carrying most of the Bibles, biblical preaching has been anything but politically articulate. Recently, a doctoral student in Chicago has been analyzing the church's response to the 1990–1991 Persian Gulf War, a war that by anyone's reading of the Christian "just war"[26] tradition must be labeled as suspect. He canvassed several American cities, telephoning ministers in the larger Protestant congregations of each city to see how they addressed the war in their sermons. Only a very small percentage of the clergy ever mentioned the war. Why? Because, as one minister put it, "We follow the lectionary here."

Though the Bible is surely hot stuff politically, apparently biblical preaching in America is not. Since the halcyon days when "God was in the White House and Eisenhower in heaven," Protestant pulpits, except for those in the African-American church, have been remarkably silent on public affairs. Probably, we must attribute the silence to a desire for calm; after all, mainline white Protestantism is often Republican and, with Presidents Nixon, Ford, Reagan, and Bush, we have preached through two decades of Republican power. Some years ago, a wonderful cartoon showed two priests eyeing an almost empty collection plate—a button, a penny, and an old "Win with Wilkie" pin. One priest is saying to the other, "Well, so much for prophecy!" Despite a reactionary political climate, must we not attribute some of the pulpit's silence to biblical preaching? Whenever some church advertises "Bible preaching" in Saturday newspapers, you know you'll be politically untroubled at best or, at worst, served up a dose of right-wing, "Word-of-God" positions. So let us argue that the rise of so-called biblical preaching has led to an ebbing of the prophetic word, at least in white Protestant churches. In America, we seem to be aiming sermons "beyond the hill of relevance."

Again: What has been the impact of so-called biblical preaching? Let us point to what might be termed *a preoccupation-with-past-tense religion*. In general, conservatives tend to look backward—they are interested in conserving the past—while revolutionaries tend to look forward with apocalyptic fervor toward some bright promised future. The biblical theology movement has been preoccupied with the historical past. After all, if revelation is in history where once upon a time God acted, preaching is bound to involve a backward look.[27] So we study our Bibles, unpacking past-tense historical revelation with historical-critical method, and fill our sermons with historical description. We picture biblical situations and then try to find situational parallels in the lives of parishioners. Of course, by preaching a God who "once upon a time" acted in history, while simultaneously denying, with Barth, any general revelation, effectively if inadvertently, we preachers have deleted God from the contemporary world. There is a kind of past-tenseness to our God, a God who was revealed long ago in something called "salvation history."[28] But where is revelation today? Today revelation is in a leather-bound book, the Holy Bible, where salvation history has been written down.[29] But the fact is, "Jesus loves me, this I know, / for the *Bible* tells me so" is not an adequate faith for grown-ups! Must preaching be past tense, or do we preach standing before a present-day, active God of our lives? We are not suggesting that Christ is not a crucial, indeed, *the* crucial disclosure of God. But we are suggesting that the *reality* of God-with-us now is the proper focus of our preaching. As Paul insists, "Now is the day of salvation."

Finally, what has been the legacy of the biblical theology movement? Let us single out a strange tension that has been building between *preaching the gospel and preaching the Bible.* Traditionally, Christian theology has insisted that the Bible contains everything necessary for salvation. In other words, the Bible may be labeled Word of God because it contains a saving gospel message. But Christian theology has seldom equated the entire Bible—every verse, every phrase—with the gospel message. Nor has Christian theology heretofore personified the entire Bible without reservation as a passionate, pursuing Word of God. As a result of an enlarging biblical conservatism, we are hearing more and more apologetic sermons trying to justify unlikely passages as being, nevertheless, Word of God.[30] We may be noticing a tension between preaching from the authority of scripture and preaching good news without any appeal to authority at all.

Some months ago we entertained a brilliant speaker on the Vanderbilt University campus. The speaker spent some forty-five minutes explaining how to preach one of those baby-bashing texts from the Hebrew scriptures, to be specific, *the* baby-bashing text, Ps. 137:9: "Happy shall they be who take your little ones and dash them against the rock!" The lecture was witty, quite brilliant, and full of homiletic insight. But when it was over, the first question from the audience was devastating. The question was, Why bother? Why would preachers bother to preach a baby-bashing text when they could be declaring the good news of the gospel? Is the whole Bible a book that must be preached simply because it is the Bible and somebody has labeled it as the Word of God? Do we preach to study particular, peculiar biblical passages, or is preaching a theological endeavor that seeks to make sense of life now in view of God's graciousness in Jesus Christ? Is not our task to preach the gospel in a difficult baby-bashing world—Bible or not? Part of the problem may have to do with a vertical notion of biblical authority. But how can we credit any sovereign biblical authority model in view of a God who is known in the outright helpless stupidity of the cross?[31] Our God is a God who seems to care more for self-giving love than for enthroned authority.

The biblical theology movement is a strange legacy. We have gained much from a golden age of historical-critical biblical scholarship. But maybe, just maybe, we have lost our homiletic souls—prophetic silence, past-tense faith, and an enlarging tension between the Bible and the good news of the gospel message.

Interpreting the Bible—Who and How

In one way, we should not blame the biblical theology movement for our hermeneutic failures. During the rise of the biblical theology movement, two cultural orientations were also on the rise: the one has been described by Philip Rieff as "the triumph of the therapeutic,"[32] and the other is a notion of truth as objective facticity.

The notion of truth as objective facticity has been around for a while. Ever since René Descartes's *cogito ergo sum* separated rational observers from a world observed, Western culture has tended to define truth empirically. As a result, perhaps particularly in America, if the Bible is true, we suppose it must be objectively true. Not everyone in America is a fundamentalist, insisting that every word in scripture must be scientifically, psychologically, and historically true.[33] Nonetheless, a lurking literalism seems to be present in the rigidities of the American religious mind that desires objective truth, particularly from a Bible that is supposed to contain historical revelation.[34] Local pastors are cautious; in competitive, numbers-game churches, they are naturally reluctant to lose members. Thus they spend an inordinate amount of time reassuring literal-minded members of their congregations about the nature of scriptural truth. (Of course, if they are Southern Baptists, their members are probably beyond reassurance. These days, Southern Baptists seem to be in a loyalty-oath situation.) Americans seem to have an odd cultural demand for objective, verifiable truth in scripture. Are there not earnest people who search for the keel of Noah's ark in the high mountains of Turkey or who try to identify some lone salt pillar as the solidification of Lot's wife? But archaeology is no substitute for theology. The question of historical actuality looms too large in the American mind and probably contributes to the misinterpretation of countless scriptural passages.

The question of literal historical truth was raised long ago in the seventeenth century by Benedict de Spinoza.[35] With the rise of rationalism as well as scientific verification, questions multiplied: Did the sun stand still for Joshua? Did the sea actually part for Moses and the children of Israel? Did Jesus stand up in a boat and tell a storm to calm down? For that matter, did Jesus rise from the dead? As a result, historical-critical method split—for some it was based on radical skepticism; for others it was dedicated to confirming the truth of the Bible. The split is still with us, particularly in America, and is exacerbated by the notion of "revelation in history." Of course, the real question can be voiced, Is the Bible a history book or is it a testimony for faith? Questions of objective facticity are almost always the wrong questions.

The other movement, "the triumph of the therapeutic," has been even more devastating. Though Freud's career bridged the nineteenth and twentieth centuries, his impact did not begin to build in America until the 1930s with the novels of Ellen Glasgow, the plays of Eugene O'Neill, and, of course, the sermons of Harry Emerson Fosdick. Most sermons from most pulpits, particularly since 1950, seem to have been aimed at an existential self in psychological self-awareness. The movement has culminated in a "positive-thinking" pulpit on the East Coast, a "possibility-thinking" pulpit on the West Coast. But the truth is that most of our pulpits, Protestant and Catholic alike, have read scripture but then preached a psychological personalism for the past four decades, with sin as psychological dysfunction and salvation as inward good feeling. No wonder that American religion can be described as both "gnosticism" and "habits of the heart."[36] Of course, the problem is that the

Bible is not addressed to selves in their isolated self-awareness. The Bible does not resonate with pool-gazing Narcissus,[37] as much as it addresses a being-saved community in the world. The true hermeneutic of scripture is ultimately *social*.

Such a statement cannot limit the interpretation of scripture; obviously the Bible can be read with reference to inner conversations—all of us seem to house a "me" and a "myself" in dialogue. What's more, the Bible can be read by Freudian psychology or Marxist ideology, by capitalism or with gnostic enthusiasms, by wealthy Western-worlders or by impoverished African or South American peoples. These many different readings may well provide rare insights. Nevertheless, we can insist that, inasmuch as the Bible is written in oral style for communities of faith, it may *intend* to be interpreted by communities of faith-seeking-understanding. If such is the case, the pretense of historical-critical objectivity on the part of a single rational interpreter may be inappropriate.

Hermeneutic questions are urgent. They cannot be dismissed as irrelevant by dogmatic Barthianism. Certainly the "critical theory" of the so-called Frankfurt school has raised concern over the validity of much white, capitalist interpretation of scripture.[38] Of course, so has recent feminist hermeneutics, the interpretations of black preaching, not to mention voices from South American, African, and Asian peoples.[39] If the Bible is addressed to marginalized people, can it be grasped by those who are both affluent and armed with power?[40] With Martin Luther, we can insist that scripture is written in a human way for human beings. Thus, theoretically the Bible is open to a very broad human interpretation. But we also can argue that the message speaks with singular joy to those who, by right of hurt or deprivation, may long for a new humanity in which to live. Those who have power, or who are well adjusted to the world, have no such longing and therefore may not be able to hear the biblical word.[41]

How have we read scripture during the height of the twentieth century? We have read the Bible as objective facticity or as a message of personal psychological salvation—"You can be a new person inside of yourself." So, though we have revered the Bible as God's Word, we seem to have ignored both its mythic depth and its social message.

The Ins and Outs of Preaching

Before we go further, let us clarify ourselves with regard to biblical preaching. We assume that evangelical, out-church preaching seldom will be overtly biblical.[42] While some popular evangelists will hold a limp Bible, announce a text, or shout out, "The Bible says . . . ," such practices are somewhat peculiar. Madison Square rallies or in-church revivals are obviously *not* the substance of evangelism. Properly speaking, evangelism is an everywhere sport. Because evangelism can happen anywhere, in a cocktail lounge as well as a church, and possibly more effectively in a cocktail lounge than a church, then the spread of the gospel is largely a lay activity without benefit of the Bible—a Bible which, in point of fact, people may know little about anyway.[43] So, in general, out-church preaching will not begin with a chunk of scripture. Instead, evangelism attempts to bring good news to human beings so that, in light of a loving God, the God disclosed in Jesus Christ crucified, their lives will take on new meaning.

But in church, when we preach to the baptized faithful, what then? Obviously in church we preach to faith-seeking-understanding, and are not merely on an evangelical fishing trip.[44] Not only do we preach to the baptized, who are joined to Jesus Christ by grace, but we also do so in the midst of worship that is "through Christ the Lord." In church, we are seeking to form God's people in faith and service, to deepen their knowledge of God through Christ Jesus, and to encourage their obedience to God's will in Christ Jesus. So, yes, we may turn to the Bible as faith seeks understanding. But, here's the question: Must we *begin* every sermon with some Bible passage? After all, we are exploring the meaning of life in view of God revealed in Christ Jesus, a task that is essentially theological. So what is the rationale for strict biblical-passage preaching in church?

Stop and think about lectionary preaching for a moment. Obviously, preaching from scriptural passages is more responsible than single-verse texts that were recommended by some of the homiletic books earlier in the century.[45] A pericope will contain some structural meaning that cannot be crammed into

15

a brief sentence or phrase. Yet, in some ways, lectionary preaching is a little like our usual church school lessons. In each case, there is an assigned hunk of scripture—say, five to ten verses. These passages are taken out of context for study. The assumption is that with a little historical research we can recover something called "original meaning" or "original situation" and in turn discover a Word of God for our lives today. The result of the assumption—namely, that every little swatch of scripture contains some sort of Word of God—is that preachers and teachers squeeze moral or spiritual meanings out of disparate passages, apparently under the illusion that any and every bit of scriptural writing contains a magic God-message.[46]

One of my grandmothers, a doughty if somewhat bigoted Christian, had a little box divided into thirty-one sections, one for each day of a month. In each section was a miniature scroll on which was printed a Bible verse. So arbitrarily you tweezered up a message from God every day. Is pericope preaching much more reliable? We have been extreme deliberately; much textual preaching has been edifying. Certainly, some Bible passages have a defined literary unity that can be interpreted on their own; for example, some parables. Nevertheless, if we examine the assumptions underlying our current fascination with pericope preaching, we may end up questioning our own sanity. Words from the Bible have no magic power. We repeat: What is the rationale for preaching a biblical passage?

The Story Remembered

Let us echo the question and grope for answers: What is the rationale for preaching a biblical passage?

Begin by arguing that any decent religion offers meaning in life. We may or may not want to suppose that human beings have Augustinian "restless hearts" or even Tillichian "ultimate concerns," but we can guess that, in unguarded moments, people do seek to make sense out of their mysterious lives. Because we human beings are born and die, because we live between memory and hope, because we have some sense of unfolding human events in which we live, meaning for us will have to be structured like a story, a story that is moving toward denouement, some *telos*. In brief, human meaning is usually found in narrative structures. Meaning must be meaning for my life and your life, lives that unfold in time, lives that we can tell like a story. Now we must be cautious; story per se is no guarantee of meaning. For example, a short, partial, slice-of-life story without a beginning or an ending, though insightful, simply cannot confer ultimate meaning. Even a story that ends with us, our identity, or our church story will not do; the story may merely reinforce our sense of ecclesial pride. Such a story will probably cheer some scholars,[47] but without wider context or ultimate purpose it can be ecclesially narcissistic. No, the story that gives meaning to life must be mythic; it must be the story of *God* and *all* humanity, a bigger narrative than our personal stories or even a Christian church story.

So what does the Bible offer? The Bible rolls out of myth and winds up in eschatological vision. What the Bible offers is narrative with an elaborate mythic beginning—creation and fall, Cain and Abel, Noah's ark, the tower of Babel. And, in the last chapters of Revelation, drawing on Ezekiel, we are offered eschatology—a Holy City with grand visions of consummation. (As an urban child, may I point out that, though the Bible begins in a garden, it ends, as it should, in a city!) In between we are given an extensive series of stories of how God has interrelated improvisationally with a recalcitrant people, Israel. These political stories, stories that begin with a bunch of visionary nomads, involve liberation from Egypt, kingship, exile, and return. So the Bible offers meaning—not in every little passage; some Bible passages may be largely irrelevant or even sub-Christian—the Bible offers meaning by handing out a story with a beginning and an end and, in between, a narrative understanding of how God may interface with our sinful humanity.

Please notice the claim we have made. We are insisting that mythic visions of origin and conclusion found in the Bible are as important as the Bible's narrativity. If we are to change people's lives, we will have to provide symbols of creation and eschaton as a framework within which story, the human

17

story, can mean. Obviously, a story without teleological conclusion will turn into meaninglessness. For human identity to be shaped by narrative, narrative must reach back before our being born, indeed before the birth of human consciousness, if it is to confer meaning. Thus, the symbols of Creation and Fall, of Cain and Abel, the rainbow and the ark, and the "religious" tower of Babel are crucial; they confer profound social meaning in which our lives may be framed. As for the composite images of conclusion that fill the final chapters of Revelation, they are a crucial poetry of meaning. Surely by depicting a churchless bivouac with God, with no more patriotism, warfare, prejudice, or hurt, the end of the Bible calls us toward God's new order.[48] But the mode of biblical storytelling is also important. As Erich Auerbach observed years ago, the Bible tells stories with dramatic brevity, unwilling to fill in the causal gaps with human motivation, precisely so that hearers may speculate the good improvisational movements of grace.[49] Biblical narrative suggests that God is ultimately the lead character in every story, including stories of politics, violence, the pious, the impious, sex, labor, and, yes, even church stories. The structure of consciousness implied in Bible stories is of course the structure of faith. Perhaps faith is formed by hearing stories.

For Christians, however, there is a kind of ultimacy in the sub-story of Jesus Christ.[50] Like a living parable,[51] Jesus Christ interprets both our human story and the story of God-with-us.[52] Obviously the gaggle of Christians way back in the first century remembered; they remembered Jesus Christ and, what's more, did so on an annual basis. Evidence certainly suggests that some sort of ritualized church year existed long before the Christian scriptures were compiled.[53] Notice: Memory work in community precedes the writing of texts. So, during the first two centuries, beginning with Easter and of course Good Friday, Christians gradually put together a patchwork church year—Epiphany, Lent, Good Friday, Holy Week, Easter, Pentecost, and perhaps a celebration of the Second Advent, anticipating the finished work of Christ. Again, please notice that such liturgical celebration *preceded* the compilation of the Christian scriptures. So let us argue that

18

preaching begins with the recollection of a story—the story of Jesus Christ set within a great God story, which the Hebrew scriptures unfold. Preaching did not begin with the Bible; no, it availed itself of the Hebrew scriptures to understand a story within a story, to grasp the meaning of a memory. Lectionaries can be helpful because they set scripture within the church's memory of Jesus Christ.[54] Of course, lectionary preaching is unhelpful if it becomes corrupted by notions of biblical authority. We are celebrating memory and not, please notice, bowing to a supposed biblical authority.

Why do we turn to scripture? To explore the remembered story of God-with-us, a story most of us began to hear long before we could hold onto a Bible.

Communities and Symbols

Again, let's repeat our question: What is the rationale for preaching a biblical passage?

We have argued that human meaning, in part, is storied and that the Bible offers us a grand narrative of God-with-us. But narrative meaning is ultimately insufficient, because meaning is also discovered in relationship. The idea goes back to George Herbert Mead and beyond. According to Mead, all of us are inwardly split: there is a "me," an acting, speaking, human being, and there is a "myself," which is formed as people act and speak to us.[55] All of which adds up to the notion of an inner self formed in relationships; we know ourselves as we are known by others in community. Psychologically, we are formed in our primary relationships within a family. Sociologically, we are shaped by communities of clan and work and friendship in which we live. Theologically, we know ourselves as we are known by a symbolically mediated God. Thus, while narratives may provide a kind of horizontal meaning in between a beginning and an end, memory and hope, there is also another kind of meaning—a vertical, ontological, meaning shaped in relationship. We seek to understand our lives in relation to God and neighbors.

The mystery of humanness is ultimately a theological

question: How can we know if God-with-us is God-for-us? Now, despite Dr. Barth's rejection of "natural theology,"[56] we are apt to consider God while brooding mysteries of the world—I'm a city street kid, but even city kids stand in awe before the sea rolling in at Coney Island or wonder at the etched loveliness of a glazed leaf in wintry Central Park. People also consider God while exploring the mystery of their own humanness; the fragility of life, we are born gasping for breath and end in ashes; the depth of life, we stare into our deep-pool selves and, though we can count twigs and leaves that may float to the surface, we can lose ourselves in the dark deeps. These are contexts in which we ask the God question, the question of meaning. The phrase "ultimate concern" echoes truth; human beings try to grasp the meaning of their lives in relation to God—and often without benefit of scripture.

But, as all good religions insist, we know God through symbols, often through symbols encountered ritually. As Christians we know God through the living symbol, Jesus Christ. He is the model of our lives, as well as source of our faith, hope, and love. The idea of Jesus Christ as a disclosure model[57] for God was built into most of us ritually long before we were able to read our Bibles. But as faith seeks to understand life with God through Jesus Christ, then we may turn to the Bible and its many symbols—covenant promises, liberation from Egypt, the thunder at Sinai, notions of kingship, the terror of exile, dreams of Zion—symbols that mediate the mystery of God in relationship. Above all, we Christian types explore the figure of Christ crucified with the sudden realization that all of us, like Nietzsche's "ugliest man,"[58] are God-killers, as well as startled recipients of amazing free grace. Paul is quite right; we no longer know Christ in a human way, for now he has become a symbol disclosing who God-for-us is and who we are before God. Christ comes to us through spoken words—at home, in church, yes, even in the world—long before we know a Bible. But as faith seeks understanding, then we may feed on scripture searching the symbol who gives meaning to our lives.

Friedrich Schleiermacher loved scripture, and yet he had nothing but scorn for people who derive religion secondhand from what he called "a dead document." "It is not the person who believes in a holy writing who has religion," he wrote, "but only the one who needs none and probably could make one for himself."[59] His words are deliberately overdrawn,[60] but they are worth considering. We have argued that the Bible serves faith-seeking-understanding. The church remembers Christ and does so through the narrative structure of the church year. What's more, the church relates to God liturgically through the symbol of Jesus Christ and has done so for centuries, indeed long before there was anything like an assembled canon. The Bible serves faith-seeking-understanding; it is seldom the source of our faith. Though we Protestants view ourselves as a "people of the Book," in actual practice the gospel message *spoken* awakens faith, and such awakening usually precedes any reference to the Bible. So scripture is secondary; scripture is something *we turn to.* Instead of embracing an authority model, perhaps we would do well to return to an early rabbinic model and view the Bible as a gift, a good gift from God to communities of faith. Authorities can dominate, but gifts to unwrap are full of delight.

A Talking God

Perhaps now we are in position to make some odd comments about preaching and Bible.

Let's begin with a bald statement: According to the Reformers, God was *Deus loquens,* a speaking God. How does God speak? Answer: *Preaching is the Word of God.* The Reformers celebrated the oral character of the gospel. Reinhold Seeberg sums up the Reformation insight:

> The Reformation . . . laid its emphasis on the word. . . . By word of God was meant primarily *not* the language of the Bible, but the orally proclaimed biblical truth.[61]

So when Martin Luther used the phrase Word of God, most of the time he was referring to preaching the gospel message, the good news of justifying grace, and not necessarily to the Bible.

"The gospel should not be something written, but a spoken word," Luther insisted.[62] John Calvin, the Reformed tradition's original whiz kid,[63] had a more comprehensive view of scripture, but was no less committed to the notion that preaching was the word of God and, further, that scripture was fulfilled not in reading, but in being preached. For Calvin, preaching was the means of God's contemporary self-revelation; the voice of the preacher preaching was the voice of God. Listen to his words (which I have cleaned up a bit to remove male generics):

> When (human beings) enter the pulpit is it so (they) may be seen from afar, so (they) may be preeminent? No, not at all. (Preachers) preach so that God may speak to us by the mouth of a (human being).[64]

In fact, it is possible to argue that Calvin grasps both scripture and preaching in the same theological pattern of thought. We are suggesting that, for the Reformers, preaching was Word of God and that, in a way, scripture was also Word of God insofar as it proclaimed the same gospel message. You see the theology in practice with the Reformed notion of a Prayer of Illumination.[65] Nowadays in many American pulpits, if there is any praying, it is apt to come directly before the sermon; after all, human words need all the praying they can get, whereas scripture is *ipso facto* considered the Word of God. But please recall that Calvin located his Prayer of Illumination prior to the reading of scripture:

> The Word itself is not quite certain for us unless it be confirmed by the testimony of the Spirit. . . . For by a kind of mutual bond the Lord has joined together the certainty of [the] Word and of [the] Spirit so that the perfect religion of the Word may abide in our minds when the Spirit, who causes us to contemplate God's face, shines. . . .[66]

Only by the working of the Spirit, through preaching, could scripture articulate a word of God. But, both the Word and the Spirit were of the Lord. And, of course, preaching was the voice of the Lord! The *Second Helvetic Confession* sums up the Reformation's view of preaching bluntly:

> *The preaching of the Word of God is the Word of God.* Wherefore when this Word of God is now preached in the church by preachers lawfully called, we believe that the very Word of God is proclaimed, and received by the faithful; and that neither any other Word of God is to be invented nor is to be expected from heaven: and that now the Word itself which is preached is to be regarded, not the minister that preaches; for even if he be evil and a sinner, nevertheless the Word of God remains still true and good.[67]

The Bible as the Word of God

Now make no mistake, the Reformers—Luther and Zwingli and Calvin—revered scripture. The slogan *sola scriptura* was clearly a Reformation battle cry. Moreover, we can quote all sorts of material to bolster the opinion that Reformers were biblical literalists and that they regarded the Bible as divine in origin. There is even considerable debate over whether the Reformers adopted a notion of "dictation" or not. But the real question is not a question of biblical authority, but rather has to do with preaching and the Bible. Did the Reformers begin with a Word-of-God Bible and then turn to speak of preaching in a secondary way, or was a rather different strategy at work?

Insofar as the Reformers affirmed the authority of scripture, they were echoing traditional Catholic teaching. In Catholic doctrine, the scriptures were holy, they were inspired by God; indeed they were God's true Word. Yes, ever since Origen in the third century, Catholic preachers had extended the interpretation of scripture to match the patterns of humanity—body, soul, and spirit; so though there was a literal, often historical meaning to the Bible's words (body), there were also extended meanings—a moral meaning (soul) and a spiritual meaning (spirit). But, in matters of dispute, St. Thomas Aquinas expresses the church's general conviction: "All these senses are founded on one—the literal—from which alone can any argument be drawn, and not from those intended in allegory."[68] What's more, there were biblical rigorists within the Catholic tradition such as Occam, who rather clearly influenced Luther's subsequent thinking. So when the Reformers chanted *sola scriptura*, they were not introducing a new biblical principle; the Catholic tradition had affirmed *scriptura* as the Word of God all along; it still does, and often in language strong enough to satisfy the most ardent modern-day fundamentalist:

> For all the books which the Church receives as sacred and canonical are written wholly and entirely, with all their parts, at the dictation of the Holy Spirit; and so far is it from being possible that any error can coexist with inspiration, that inspiration not only is essentially incompatible with error, but excludes and rejects it as absolutely and necessarily as it is impossible that God Himself, the supreme Truth, can utter that which is not true. This is the ancient and unchanging faith of the Church, solemnly defined in the Councils of Florence and Trent, and finally confirmed and more expressly formulated by the Council of the Vatican. (From the Encyclical Letter of Pope Leo XIII, *Providentissimus Deus* [1893])[69]

The Reform in the Reformation

So what was new in the Reformation? What was new was the word *sola!* The word *sola* demoted pronouncements of the papacy and the teachings of tradition. Early on, surely since the time of Irenaeus, Catholic thinking had insisted that properly the tradition of the church should guide the interpretation of scripture so that, by the time of the Reformation, the church had added to the scriptural norm a famous *et*, scripture *and* tradition.[70] Instead, the Reformers set up scripture *alone*—that is, scripture scripturally self-interpreted—as authority in the church. When Reformers spoke of the inspired authority of scripture, they were echoing ancient church tradition. But when they added the word *sola*, they were being uniquely Protestant.

Of course, it was inevitable that the *sola,* which encouraged the study of the Bible, would eventually come into conflict with inherited medieval notions of inspired *scriptura.* The tension certainly shows up early in the thought of the Reformers themselves. Luther raised questions about biblical veracity: He notes errors in prophetic writings, he questions the authorship of Genesis, he doubts that Solomon wrote Ecclesiastes, he criticizes doctrine in the letter to the Hebrews, he would drop Esther and James out of the canon, etc.[71] And, though Calvin was more conservative with respect to the whole Bible, in his commentaries he too noted errors, and he too was troubled by some of the books in the canon, notably the Apocalypse and the Song of Songs. James Barr is helpfully blunt:

> The Reformation never had the answer to the problem of biblical exegesis. On the contrary, the Reformation position was an inherently unstable one, which produced some magnificent insights and results but which equally bequeathed to the succeeding generations sets of antinomies and aporias which have troubled us ever since. To quote the most obvious, it put us on the road which led towards a full biblical criticism on the one hand, and at the same time on the road which led to fundamentalism on the other.[72]

So the Reformers embraced a *static* notion of biblical authority—a notion that was subsequently intensified by post–Reformation confessions such as the Westminster Confession of Faith—while at the same time endorsing a literal, historical approach to the study of texts.[73]

Things in Their Places

What can we say of the Reformation witness? The problem with revisiting the Reformers is that almost anything can be proved by citation. But doctrine should be analyzed in relationship to other doctrines. Generally, the Reformers celebrated the authority of the Bible. In cheering the authority of scripture, they were echoing what had been conventionally stated by medieval theology. The question we must ask is how did they frame their discussions of scripture as the Word of God—where was the doctrine *placed?*

First, let us suggest that behind the notion of biblical authority they inherited from medieval Catholicism is another authority: Jesus Christ. The *real* authority for Reformers is the gospel message of Jesus Christ. To capture the essence of the Reformation, *solus Christus* is a better slogan. For Luther, the scriptures are Word of God because they contain Christ the Savior. Writing of the Hebrew scriptures, Luther is quite explicit:

> "Here you will find the swaddling cloths and the manger in which Christ lies. . . . [S]imple and lowly are these swaddling cloths, but dear is the treasure, Christ, who lies in them."[74]

His words could apply with equal conviction to the entire Bible. Surely, his somewhat cavalier treatment of James— "One of these days I'll use Jimmy to light the fire!"—is based on a christological judgment, for though James may mention the name of Jesus, the letter has no developed Christology.[75] Philip Watson, a splendid interpreter of Luther, sums up Luther's understanding of authority:

> [F]or Luther, all authority belongs ultimately to Christ, the Word of God, alone, and even the authority of the Scriptures is secondary and derivative, pertaining to them only inasmuch as they bear witness to Christ and are the vehicle of the Word.[76]

Calvin is more cautious than Luther in his treatment of scripture, but his definition of Word of God is no less christological. Listen to Calvin on scripture:

> This is what we should . . . seek in the whole of Scripture: truly to know Jesus Christ, and the infinite riches that are comprised in him and are offered to us by him from God the Father. If one were to sift thoroughly the Law and the Prophets, [he/she] would not find a single word which

would not draw and bring us to him. And for a fact, since all the treasures of wisdom and understanding are hidden in him, there is not the least question of having, or turning toward, another goal. . . .[77]

In other words, for the Reformers, scripture's value was that it declared the saving good news of Jesus Christ. Ultimately, the true authority of the Reformers was our Lord and Savior Jesus Christ crucified! They discovered a knowledge of God through Jesus Christ in the Bible. They recognized the liberating good news of gospel which in fact had liberated them![78]

Second, their understanding of the Word of God in scripture is *oral.* We have already mentioned the Reformers' stress on the oral character of God's Word and the use by God of broken human voices. To the Reformers, the Bible was God's Word because it was *preaching,* God's preaching. They do not refer much to the Bible as writing, but rather as God's speaking. So the model in which the Bible is understood is an oral model. No wonder that Luther could write:

The Gospel should really not be something written, but a spoken word. . . . This is why Christ himself did not write anything but only spoke. He called his teaching not Scripture but gospel, meaning good news or a proclamation that is spread not by pen but by word of mouth.[79]

Luther can be extreme in his reverence for the oral word of the gospel message preached. Consider:

Someone once asked Luther, "Doctor, is the word that Christ spoke when he was on earth the same in fact and in effect as the word preached by a minister?" "Yes," Luther replied, "because he said, 'He who hears you hears me . . .'"[80]

By contrast, again and again Luther implies that the writing of books is a necessary evil.

In many ways, Calvin is just as committed to the oral declaration of the gospel:

Though the Law was written, yet God would have the living voice always to resound in (the) Church, just as today. The Scripture is conjoined with preaching as by an invisible bond.[81]

But more telling are Calvin's many, many phrases defending the Bible as Word of God, almost all of which use oral imagery:

For Calvin, in practice, the whole Bible is the Word of God: the expressions "Scripture says" and "The Holy Spirit says" are used synonymously (passim). In the Scriptures God "opens his own most hallowed lips," and we are certain that they come to us "from the very mouth of God." Hence Calvin introduces his exposition of the Ten Commandments with the invitation: "Now let us hearken to God himself as he speaks in his own words."[82]

Calvin seems to use much the same language when he discusses preaching; preaching is also the voice of God. Like Luther, Calvin also cites Luke 10:16, "He who hears you hears me, and he who rejects you rejects me." Preachers, according to Calvin, are "the very mouth of God."[83] Those who suppose that a private reading of the Bible is sufficient and therefore deem preaching to be superfluous are roundly condemned.[84] Calvin's entire theological system is laced with references to preaching: Preaching is the means of God's election, the voice of God's judgment and absolution, the means of our saving union with Christ, the way God governs the church. In sum, Calvin calls the pulpit God's throne *(le siege)*.[85]

Does Calvin affirm a primacy of the *preached* message of the gospel, as did Luther? No. Basically, he sees preaching as an expounding of God's message in scripture, although he does suggest that, in particular, faith rests on the gospel promises.[86] So, though Calvin clearly affirms the authority of Jesus Christ, our only mediator, and celebrates the preaching of Christ as the chief means of saving grace, he has not brought these convictions to bear on traditional notions of biblical authority.[87] But, the underscoring of God's Word as an oral address is still evident in Calvin's thinking, as is his high, holy doctrine of preaching.

The ambiguity in Calvin's thought still lives in churches of the Reformed tradition: Is the Bible in its totality the Word of God? Or is the Bible Word of God because it contains the good news of God, which is redemptive and in fact is the substance of preaching? Of late, many preachers seem to have opted for the first statement to the neglect of the second.

Our Biblical Captivity

In our century, Reformation understandings seem to have reversed. Authority is lodged in scripture, and preaching seems to be a secondary activity, an adjunct to scripture. Thus, to us, preaching is a word of God only insofar as it begins with and interprets a scriptural text. Baldly we have reversed the Reformation pattern without realizing it. Perhaps we have wanted to run away from the high theology of our Reformation forebears—"The preaching of the Word of God is the Word of God." To borrow Fred Craddock's apt phrase, we have preferred to preach "as one without authority."[88] After all, the whole notion of being the voice of God is, to say the least, somewhat intimidating. To most of us, the idea smacks of domination. We tend to think of thundering Scottish speech from high-hung Presbyterian pulpits. But no, we misunderstand. According to scripture, God spoke through a decidedly odd collection of people—through an impulsive, often inarticulate Moses; through David, the Mayor Daley of Israel; through prophets, some of whom may have been quite loony (surely Ezekiel was diagnosable); and others painfully self-pitying (recall Elijah cowering in a cave). According to the Christian scriptures, God also spoke through the voice of Apostles, a mixed bag at best. Remember Peter's cry, "We too are human beings with the same passions as you" (Acts 14:15). So, the issue is not dominance. After all, do we not speak for a God who was revealed in the sheer helplessness of Christ crucified? The authority model is dispensable; speaking for God in our brokenness is not. Crypto-fundamentalism may elevate scripture and denigrate preaching, but why should we, children of the Reformation, countenance such an error?

Let us be clear: We are arguing for a church animated by the gospel, rather than a church heavily under the rule of an imposed scriptural authority. Nowadays people seem to suppose that, to be labeled "kosher," every sermon *has* to begin with scripture or else it will tip toward heresy or, even worse, theological liberalism! Are only those sermons that unravel from scriptural pericopes rightly labeled word of God? Such a supposition seems to be based on a somewhat groundless notion of biblical authority—"Scripture is recognized as the Word of God by the fact that it *is* the Word of God." John Fry satirizes the lust for authority in the church as a slogan: "The New Testament Says the Apostles Say God Says the Gospel Is the Word of God."[89] The Bible is surely a good gift from God, and Christian people may (and should) feed with pleasure on its words every day. The Bible is a good gift because it can deepen our knowledge of God; and the knowledge of God through Jesus Christ is surely a sweet saving knowledge. But if the Bible's authority becomes separated from the gift of salvation—if biblical authority stands apart from Jesus Christ, and the scriptures are accorded some sort of intrinsic divinity by Christian communities—then the Bible can imprison preaching's lively word. Please recall that early Christians preached good news without having a fixed canon and, despite a less than compelling meeting at Jamnia, did so without any developed notion of an authoritative Bible. Is it possible that the God of Jesus Christ may not need our biblical protectiveness? What the God of Jesus Christ does desire is preaching—prophetic, passionate, theologically considered preaching of good news, the good news that calls us into God's new humanity and sets us free to live!

Why is preaching a "Word of God?" Preaching is a word of God *only* if it serves God's redemptive purposes. Preaching announces good news of the gospel and, in so doing, sets people free for God's new humanity. Preaching is not a word of God because it is under church auspices. Preaching is not a word of God because it speaks from a "warmed heart." And preaching is not a word of God because it draws on a biblical passage. No, preaching is only a word of God if, instigated by the Spirit, it serves God's redemptive purpose. But please note: The same argument may be transferred to scripture! Is the Bible the Word of God? Yes, the Bible is lofty literature. And, yes, it gathers a noble assembly of religious voices representing thousands of years of faith. But can the Bible be Word of God when it is used to demean women, inflame prejudice, or bash members of the gay/lesbian community? With both scripture and preaching "in use," activity is the test. Neither preaching nor scripture is Word of God per se. The Bible *can be* God's Word because it can speak redemptively. Otherwise, the Bible is no more than a distinguished literary compendium. When God speaks, the Word of God is freedom.

The rearranging of Bible and preaching is more urgent than we guess. Don't we realize that a four-hundred-year "book culture" is drawing to a close?[90] Oh, there will still be books, and there will be language to read—whether it's on a page or a computer screen or some other electronic system. What's more, we will still have Bibles, bound or unbound, for us to feed on. No, the big problem, as Neil Postman has seen clearly, is that a kind of epistemology of the printed page will be replaced by an epistemology of electric media.[91] In other words, people will no longer think in bookish/rational patterns of thought, but rather will think in ways that are formed by the electronic devices that they use and that use them. All of which is to say that it will be almost impossible to retain a book-authority mentality in the forthcoming twenty-first century. Such a shift may seem to threaten our modern-day Protestantism, particularly Reformed Protestantism, with its strong cry of *sola scriptura*. We Protestants have labeled ourselves "people of the Book," but in an electronic age will the slogan become an anachronism? Because clocks cannot turn back a century at a time, rather obviously, Protestant understandings of "Word of God" will have to be revised—and revised in an oral direction.

So let us reaffirm our heritage: Preaching is God's Word to us. Preaching is the Word of God because it functions within God's liberating purpose and *not* necessarily because it is per se biblical. All along, God has wanted to be one with humanity. So the voice of preaching speaks God's love to the world. Of course, if human beings are to be free in communion with God, then preaching must participate in God's redemptive purposes as well. Can we be bold? We do not preach for the sake of the church. We do not preach so the Bible will be known and highly regarded. We do not preach for any reason except that God has called us and seeks to use our voices for the liberation of humanity. So when we preach God's redemptive word, guess what? Our voices, our piping little sin-struck, frightened, underpaid, hesitant voices just happen to be the voice of God. Imagine that—please, oh please, imagine that!

2

Preaching and Church

There is a Catholic church where an enormous painting, high as a house, fills a chancel wall. It is a picture of risen, victorious Jesus Christ. Perhaps the artist was trying to illustrate a verse from Revelation, because he painted Christ—Alpha and Omega—with an outsized two-edged sword coming from his mouth.[1] The sword points down so that, if you are seated in church, it seems to be pointing directly at you. Who are we who gather Sunday after Sunday in church buildings? We are people addressed by the sharp, two-edged word of Christ:

> Indeed, the word of God is living and active, sharper than any two-edged sword; piercing until it divides soul from spirit, joints from marrow; it is able to judge the thoughts and intentions of the heart. (Heb. 4:12)

Now here's a question: These days, have we inadvertently turned the sword the other way around?

The Astonishing Power of Preaching

Let us begin by leafing our Bibles: The Christian scriptures have a huge confidence in preaching. The apostle Paul, the

33

Gospel writers, even the so-called catholic epistles—they all celebrate the power of preaching. And why not? The earliest Christians were good Jews; they knew that God spoke, "Let there be light," and the world was created. They were sure that, as the world spins and seasons change, patterns of nature are ordered by God's command. Listen to Ps. 147:15–18:

> He sends out his command to the earth;
>   his word runs swiftly.
> He gives snow like wool;
>   he scatters frost like ashes.
> He hurls down hail like crumbs—
>   who can stand before his cold?
> He sends out his word, and melts them;
>   he makes his wind blow, and the waters flow.

But the same word of God that rules creation also speaks to God's own people of ethical responsibility. The psalm continues (vv. 19–20):

> He declares his word to Jacob,
>   his statutes and ordinances to Israel.
> He has not dealt thus with any other nation;
>   they do not know his ordinances.

As good Jews, early Christians were quite sure that whatever God spoke would be, for God's word could never end in futility; God's word did what God said. In a way, the word *was* God's power:

> For as the rain and the snow come down from
>   heaven,
>   and do not return there until they have
>   watered the earth,
> making it bring forth and sprout,
>   giving seed to the sower and bread to the eater,
> so shall my word be that goes out from my mouth;
>   it shall not return to me empty,
> but it shall accomplish that which I purpose,
>   and succeed in the thing for which I sent it.
>   (Isa. 55:10–11)

So God's word, *dabar*, was always an expression of God's purpose; it *did* what God intended and did so with power. Life and death, prosperity and poverty, suffering and health—all were determined by the word of the Lord God. In the Christian scriptures, Paul the apostle clearly believes in the power of God's word, the same word that created the heavens and the earth. For Paul echoes God's first word in creation, "Let there be light;" through preaching, he contends, we get light, "the light of the knowledge of God in the face of Christ Jesus" (2 Cor. 4:6). To Paul, preaching was filled with the huge creative power of God.

But preaching was also knowledge—"the *knowledge* of God . . . ." Preaching disclosed the hidden-in-mystery nature of God to God's elect people. The early Christians remembered how God gave a word to prophets, vision to dazzle Ezekiel's eyes, a coal on the lips of awed Isaiah. Again and again, sections of the Hebrew scriptures begin, "The Word of the Lord came to . . ." The phrase "Word of the Lord" shows up nearly five hundred times, for, according to the Hebrew Bible, God spoke to Abraham, Moses, Elijah, Elisha, to Jeremiah again and again, to Ezekiel, Hosea, Micah, Zephaniah, Malachi, and many, many others. The God of the Bible speaks through chosen preachers and speaks prophetically. What does the word of the Lord have to say? The word of the Lord always recalls God's covenant love and at the same time pictures God's purposes—the great, good vision of Zion. In between, Israel is called to trusting faith as well as social ethics. Preaching, prophetic preaching, is a gift that God gives to Israel:

> Therefore my people shall know my name; therefore in that day, they shall know that it is I who speak; here am I.

> How beautiful upon the mountains
> are the feet of the messenger
> who announces peace,
> who brings good news,
> who announces salvation,
> who says to Zion, "Your God reigns."
> (Isa. 52:6–7)

35

Echoing the words of Isaiah, Paul the apostle insists that preaching is all-important. He recites a series of questions:

> For "Everyone who calls on the name of the Lord will be saved." But how are they to call on one in whom they have not believed? And how are they to believe in one of whom they have never heard? And how are they to hear without someone to proclaim him? And how are they to proclaim him unless they are sent? As it is written, "How beautiful are the feet of those who bring good news!". . . So faith comes from what is heard, and what is heard comes through the word of Christ. (Rom. 10:13–17)

Let us begin by acknowledging the Bible's sure confidence in the Word preached. The Word of God declared is power and wisdom; the same unexpected power and wisdom found in the impotent foolishness of the *saving* cross of Jesus Christ.

Preaching: Out-Church and In

In Christian scriptures, preaching is subdivided. The primary mode of preaching is obviously evangelical; we preach to the world. Study the resurrection stories that end our Gospels;[2] according to Willi Marxsen, they all contain evangelical commissionings.[3] Remember the white-robed gent who shows up in the Gospel of Mark; he urges women at the tomb to go and tell good news. The same story is picked up and repeats with variations in Matthew and Luke—"Go tell," the angels say to women at the tomb (which incidentally authenticates the ordination of women preachers, angelic authority being somewhat higher than the courts of the church). Of course, Matthew adds another commissioning when he has the risen Christ perched on a mountain telling his followers to hustle off and make disciples of all nations.[4] Still later, Luke has Christ command a "preaching of repentance and the forgiveness of sins" to all people.[5] Even the peculiar Gospel of John features a commissioning: "As the Father has sent me, so I send you." Yes, according to Luke, Jesus had previously dispatched seventy disciples to preach in his name,[6] but then came the cross and his disciples scattered. With resurrection, the community came to life again and was recommissioned by a risen Christ. "Go tell . . . ," the words define our evangelical task; we are to tell good news to the world.

But, stop and notice, the same resurrection stories contain mention of the church's common life. In the resurrection stories are references to forgiveness (possibly a ritual action), the breaking of bread, the incorporation of baptism, and, above all, to preaching within the community of faith.[7] Just as risen Christ taught his disciples for forty days, there must be continuing instruction within the community of faith.[8] So in Luke's story of the Emmaus road, the risen Christ stops right in the middle of the road and, of all things, delivers a formal Christian sermon, interpreting [*diermēneusen*] the scriptures from "Moses and all the prophets."[9] And what about the white-robed chap in the Gospel of Mark? Could he be the same person who ran from the Garden of Gethsemane without his pants? Stripped naked—exposed as a sinner by the death of Christ—is he now a white-robed, baptized, Christian preacher announcing the gospel message to the church: "He is not here; he is risen!"?[10] Certainly the Gospel of John chides skeptical Thomas for refusing to believe the preaching of his fellow disciples on the Lord's Day.[11] So the biblical record contains two kinds of preaching; there is out-church preaching that proclaims good news to the world and there is in-church preaching that shapes the community in faith and hope and love. After all, Christian community must be a sign of the new order, as well as salt and light for the world.

There's something else to notice in the resurrection materials: apocalyptic imagery. There are white-robed angelic messengers, an empty tomb, a gravestone tossed around like tiddledywinks, a last trumpet, and even the newly risen dead cakewalking the streets of Jerusalem! The stories feature symbols of an apocalyptic future suddenly come true. Thus they hint at the crux of the gospel message, namely, that God's new age has begun, the "kingdom has come." What do you do when you find yourself in a new social order? Why, you repent and believe, that is, completely change the patterns of your life so as to live in a new way. The resurrection was interpreted through apocalyptic symbols precisely because of its cosmic significance: The second Adam had appeared and a new humanity had begun on earth! No wonder the church is called to preach evangelically; we are to announce God's new order. And, at the same time, we must form ourselves in faith; we who are in Christian community are called to display some sign of God's new order.

Now, underline an affirmation: According to scripture, all preaching, in-church or out-church, is empowered by God. Ultimately, preaching is God's word, not our word. At the beginning of 1 Corinthians, Paul sets up a series of daring analogies. By anyone's reckoning, he says, Christ crucified was both impotent and foolish; nevertheless, Christ crucified was the power and wisdom of God in action. Likewise, the church is weak and stupid, without smarts or cash or social status—not displaying "Lifestyles of the Rich and Famous"; but the church is also filled with the hidden, unassuming power of God so that, if Christians boast, they must "boast in the Lord." Finally, Paul picks on preaching, which he describes as "weakness and fear and much trembling" without "plausible words of wisdom." Yet, nonetheless, preaching is full of God's own power and wisdom. So preaching, in-church or out, our fallible, foolish preaching is full of God's hidden redemptive power! There's a church in Ohio with a sign on the back side of its pulpit that only those who preach can see. You step into the pulpit and read: "Remember, please, you speak God's word." Look, we may be skeptical, we may even be reluctant to preach—ever since Jeremiah most preachers are—but please acknowledge the Bible's astonishing confidence in the preached word of God.

A Look at the Reformers

Now, skip a bunch of years and drop in on the sixteenth-century Protestant Reformers. The Reformation saw a renewed confidence in preaching. The Reformers, like all good revolutionaries, were absolutely convinced of the power of speech—free, brave, godly speech. After all, didn't the Reformers set the preached word of God over the pronouncements of church authority. Of all things, they set an ordinary pulpit up against the papacy. Of course, they believed that preaching, instigated by the Holy Spirit, was truly God's word. Just as the Spirit of God visited ancient prophets and gave them speech, so contemporary preachers were empowered by the same prophetic Spirit.[12] Moreover, the Spirit of God also worked inwardly in the hearts of believers to attest the truth of the Word.[13]

> [Christ] will be of no benefit to you and you will not be able to avail yourself of him unless God translates him into words whereby you can hear and know him. . . . He must be brought to you, prepared for you, and translated into words for you by means of the inner and external Word.[14]

Without the power of the Holy Spirit, they argued, preaching would be emptiness.

In speaking of the Word and the Spirit, the Reformers were developing a Trinitarian analogy. Just as Word and Spirit were one in the Triune God, so Word and Spirit were one, working together in preaching and hearing the gospel. Wherever the Word was rightly declared, there the Spirit was at work. And whenever people responded in the Spirit, then truly a Word of God had been spoken. Remember Paul's rough quip to the bone-headed Galatians: "Did you get the Spirit," Paul asks, "by doing works of the law, or by faith-hearing?"[15] So, though the Spirit prompted preaching, the Word preached formed the Spirit with the community. And, in turn, the Spirit with the community received and believed the Word. The Word, of course, was a verbal incarnation; it was Christ come to us. According to the Reformers, preaching was a gift from the great Triune God.

What about in-church and out-church preaching? Though the Reformers did not use such categories, in an indirect way they kept the distinction. Probably Luther and Calvin were trapped in a Christendom model so that it was difficult for them to conceive of an "out-church" world. Yes, there were

Jews and Muslims to convert, and certainly there were erroneous sectarians to correct, but by and large the Reformers seemed to have almost no sense of a wider secular world awaiting news of the gospel.[16] Possibly they were too concerned with reform to think in wider ways. Nevertheless, they indirectly distinguished between preaching that could set the sinner free in justifying grace and preaching to sanctify the holy people of God. Luther, leery of any preaching that might urge works of the law, avoided extensive discussions of sanctification and instead asked for a regular reiteration of the good news of justification by grace, a message that he believed would convert continually. But the distinction is still very much in Luther's thought:

> [S]anctification, once begun, daily increases, [for] the Holy Spirit is continually at work in us, by means of the Word of God, and daily bestowing forgiveness on us, till we reach that life where there is no more forgiveness, all persons there being pure and holy.[17]

Calvin, though he believed justification and sanctification proceeded together from our union with Christ, nonetheless saw two modes of preaching; a justifying word that set a soul free for God and a sanctifying word that formed the people of God in holiness.[18] Though we may be correct in criticizing the Reformers—they did lack proper missionary concern—nevertheless they seem to have distinguished two types of preaching, the same two types of preaching found in biblical thought. There was preaching to liberate captive sinners and there was preaching to form the community in holy faith.

But, in the thought of the Reformers, God's word is set *over* the church. The church is subservient to the preached Word of God.

> [The Lord] alone should rule and reign in the church as well as have authority or pre-eminence in it, and this authority should be exercised and administered by his Word alone. Nevertheless . . . we have said that he uses the ministry of [people] to declare openly his will to us by mouth, as a sort of delegated work, not by transferring to them his

right and honor, but only that through their mouths he may do his own work—just as a [worker] uses a tool to do . . . work.[19]

Calvin is quite emphatic: "The power of the church," he writes, "is not unlimited, but is subject to the Word of God."[20] His reasoning is clear: How else can Christ be head of the church unless Christ speaks with a contemporary voice. Therefore, ministers must be trained in scripture and in theology so that, in Calvin's words, they "speak from the mouth of the Lord."[21] "Why do we come to the sermon?" asks Calvin, ". . . It is that God may govern us and that we may have our Lord Jesus Christ as sovereign teacher."[22]

Through preaching, then, God in Christ brings judgment on the church and, at the same time, the message of absolution. Calvin urges preachers to use vigor and *vivacité* in speaking to empower God's word, though he realizes that such preaching may not be terribly popular. Listen to dialogue from one of Calvin's sermons:

What! Is this the way to teach? Ho! We want to be won by sweetness. . . . You do? Then go and teach God his lessons! . . . Ho! We want to be taught in another style. . . . Well then, go to the devil's school! He will flatter you enough—and destroy you.[23]

God's judgment comes upon the church through preaching. But God's word of mercy also is given to the church from the pulpit:

[W]hen the whole church stands, as it were, before God's judgment seat, confesses itself guilty, and has its sole refuge in God's mercy, it is no common or light solace to have present there the ambassador of Christ, armed with the mandate of reconciliation, by whom it hears pronounced its absolution.[24]

In Calvin's thought, the Word of God is enthroned over the church through the words of preachers.

41

As for Luther, his claims are as sweeping. Through the preached Word God gathers the church, and through the same Word God directs the church:

> Since the church owes its birth to the Word, is nourished, aided, and strengthened by it, it is obvious it cannot be without the Word. If it is without the Word, it ceases to be a Church.[25]

As with Calvin, God's word to the church is both judgment and mercy, law and grace. The spiritual use of the law, according to Luther, is to "increase transgressions," or, better, an awareness of our transgressions, so that we may receive consolations of the gospel message eagerly:

> [T]he work of God is twofold, namely proper and strange, so also the office of the gospel is twofold. The proper office of the gospel is to proclaim the proper work of God, i.e. grace. . . . But the strange work of the gospel is to prepare a people perfect for the Lord, that is, to reveal sins and to pronounce guilty those that were righteous in their own eyes. . . .[26]

Ultimately, for Luther, the Word does everything in the church. Of course, Luther understands that word aligns with a "theology of the cross," whereas other forms of power do not:

> Speech is a great and divine gift. It is with words and not with might that wisdom rules [people], instructs, edifies, consoles and soothes in all circumstances of life, especially in affairs of conscience. Therefore God provided [the] church with audible preaching. . . . The power of the oral word is truly remarkable.[27]

Why is preaching so important? Because the character of the church is shaped by preaching. Again and again, preaching calls the church to repentance. And, again and again, the absolution of God comes through preaching. So preaching forms the Spirit of the church, a church that is ever judged and forgiven by Christ the Lord. But more, the church is also directed in its purposes by the Word and the Spirit. The Reformers, with strange bravado, set the voice of preaching up over the church.

The Revolt of the Congregation

Question: Have we reversed the two-edged sword?

The Reformers saw preaching as a two-edged sword wielded by the risen Christ. The church is called by Christ, ordered by Christ, and, because it is comprised of willful, forgiven sinners, the church lives under both the judgment and sweet mercy of Christ. Preaching is always a reiterated Declaration of Pardon. But, somehow, have we turned the sword around? In our day, has preaching become subservient to the church? A good theologian, Langdon Gilkey, said it neatly: "Protestantism unseated the pope, not in order to replace him by the congregation, but to enthrone Jesus Christ, the Word of God, there."[28] Has the congregation gradually become our ultimate authority?

You can see the turnaround in little ways. Certainly some exponents of liturgical renewal tend to regard the sermon as an enemy of true liturgy. Of course, in a way they are quite right, because spotlighted, center-stage pulpiteering can destroy our common worship. Did the famous definition of preaching, "truth through personality," encourage preaching as a dramatic art?[29] Certainly we all have seen appalling displays of pulpit posturing, soliloquies of unintended bathos, that have turned off faith. Because preaching does bring us Christ, the living Word, in-church preaching properly should occur in the context of worship. In worship we hear and respond to the Word with praise; we know Christ in a new way, not merely as historical hearsay, but relationally as our common Lord and Savior. Theodore Jennings argues that Christ's absence—"He is not here; he is risen"—is the basis of Christian worship.[30] Worship begins in gratitude, for we are liberated people;[31] but worship is also filled with "Lord come!" longing, as we look for the consummation of Christ's reconciling work.

The sacrament of the Lord's Supper, following the preaching of the Word, shows the shape of Christ's saving work in advance; eucharist is "future-present."[32] So, real eucharistic presence is a presence in promise and therefore a real presence-in-absence.[33] Clearly, preaching within the community of faith does belong in the context of praise.

A deeper truth: Without worship, and singularly without eucharist, preaching is ever undercut by doubt. For if in preaching we announce a new humanity raised up on the earth, descended by faith from Jesus Christ, the second Adam, people are bound to be skeptical. Where is such a new humanity in our truly inhumane world? And where is the new humanity in church, a church often guilty of riveting every dear, dreamed human hope to the past? Wasn't it Adolf Harnack who wryly observed that though Jesus announced a "kingdom of God," the church arrived instead?[34] In free-church, non-eucharistic communities, the good news of the gospel is ever undercut by the obvious absence of a kingdom of God as well as the chronic self-righteousness of us religious people. So what is the solution? Should we impose moral restrictions to shape up our congregations? No, for then the church, coerced by law, will end up in contradiction to the good-grace gospel message.[35] Instead, if the Lord's Supper is a context for our speaking, people will hear the gospel and find themselves within a real, physically formed, living sign of the gospel promise, the shape of things to come.[36] In a gathered-at-table family of God, beyond politics, or race, or sex, or privilege, we can believe the good news we have heard preached. Clearly, in-church preaching ought to be at table. Barth is quite right to insist that proper preaching should be "accompanied and explained by the sacraments." He is doubly right when he criticizes his own Reformed tradition: "What kind of preaching is it that receives its prominence from suppression of the sacraments . . . ?"[37] Preaching and worship belong together.

But, on the other hand, is preaching merely *part* of the liturgy, a component, one among many, provided by a salaried, well-vested, court-prophet clergy? And should preaching be ruled by something elusive that many ministers seem to label "liturgical mood"?[38] If preaching is merely a liturgical component, and liturgy in turn is merely an expression of the church's faith, then—guess what?—preaching is suddenly demoted; it is no longer God's two-edged sword.[39] "Liturgy" means a public work of the people;[40] but is preaching something we people both originate and perform? There remains a peculiar, probably unresolvable, tension between preaching and worship that we must acknowledge.[41] According to the Reformers, the word of God through preaching is always *extra nos,* a word from God that we ourselves do not and indeed cannot possess. Yes, a right pattern of worship is *Wort* and *Antwort,* word and response, and within such a pattern, sermons are intended to be *Wort,* God's address to a people, though conducted with modesty and in what is often a somewhat dialogical style. But style is no substitute for theology. The tension between preaching and liturgy is ultimately a tension between God's immediate word to us and the regularities of our liturgical praise. Theologically the tension is somewhat eased by the realization that all worship is instigated by God's Word and Spirit. So, though in-church preaching should occur in worship and should be braced by sacraments, Baptism and the Lord's Supper, preaching nevertheless must not be regarded as merely one component among many in liturgy—versicles, hymns, readings, sermons, creeds, and so forth.

Preaching is larger than liturgy because it happens beyond liturgy as well as within liturgy; indeed, preaching is the *kerygma* that has called forth liturgy. Lately, there is a tendency to subsume preaching under the heading "liturgy," and in turn to regard liturgy as an expression of the church's faith. In such a scheme, preaching is congregational self-expression that clergy, with democratic concern, can articulate.[42] But preaching is not simply a word that emerges from the faith of a people, or that is received from a flow of tradition; presumably preaching is in some sense "God's voice." Preachers are responsible to the God revealed in Christ Jesus who is surely the true head of the church.

Please do not misunderstand: Preachers are church people. They themselves hear the saving gospel from the church, a gospel they too will speak. "There is no salvation apart from the church," was a Reformation watchword. But we must be precise; we are not saved *by* the church, and we are not saved by being *in* the church. No, we are saved by God's grace alone, through faith, and faith is formed by hearing the spoken gospel. But we must not suggest that ministers declare the *church's* message or that they are servants of the church per se. Ministers are called by God *through* the voice of the church, but they are nonetheless the servants of God. The church is not an ultimate, but the good news of God is. There is an amusing story of Philipp Melanchthon and Luther. The Zwickau "prophets," charismatic preachers, came along, and Melanchthon was quite taken with their piety. But, cautious, he wrote to Luther asking his opinion. Luther suggests that they be tested; Melanchthon should ask them about their call. If they say their call came directly from God, then, says Luther, "I definitely do not want them to be accepted." For, according to Luther, "God has never sent anyone, not even the Son himself, unless he was called *through* [people]."[43] To Luther, God's call came *through* the church, but was not reducible to a call of the church, simply because the church is *not* Christ. In a time such as our own when God seems strangely absent, we tend to overinvest our faith in the church. But in the thought of the Reformers, the Word of God preached, although of the church, was emphatically over the church and, incidentally, over preachers as well.

In the Religious "Marketplace"

Of course, these days, preaching may be demoted by the necessities of church promotion. Churches seem to rise or fall according to marketing techniques—all under the deceptive banner of evangelism or, perhaps, the catchphrase "managed church growth." As a result, we have turned ministers into ecclesial entrepreneurs. Call it the triumph of Lyle Schaller theology—that is, if the phrase "Lyle Schaller theology" isn't an oxymoron.[44] If you are competing for souls in a religious "marketplace," then preaching can be taken over by a notion of congregational preference. If congregations want therapy, let's preach therapy. If they hanker for a handout of self-esteem, let sermons be upbeat!

In a recent "Doonesbury" cartoon panel, a church-shopping young couple is appalled to hear a preacher use the word "sinners." "We're looking for a church that's supportive, a place where we can feel good about ourselves," the young wife explains.[45] In a church-management model, the congregation, its needs, its pluralism, its incipient faith can reduce preaching to a "positive," house-organ voice. At a time when mainline denominations seem to be struggling for survival, preaching can be ordered by extravagant fantasies of church growth.[46] Let's preach whatever the pollsters tell us the American soul craves. Question: Has Christ's two-edged sword been handed over to the congregation in our age? Answer: Perhaps.

Let us assume that a definition of ministry will determine the character of preaching. In Calvin's mind, the preacher was to be a voice for God, and therefore, of necessity, preachers were to be brainy theologians, exegetes, and teachers—not to mention God-obsessed! But nowadays, the term of choice seems to be "enabler"; ministers are to be enablers for a congregation.[47] Now the concept of the enabler has virtues; it acknowledges that ministry is something in which we are all engaged. By baptism, all of us have been ordained to a common ministry. But examine the term more closely; the word enabler seems to mean in two primary ways. An enabler can be a person who removes inhibitions, blocks, hangups so that people may be free for self-fulfillment; thus, it can have a therapeutic meaning. Or, in our world today, an enabler can be an executive who manages a corporate body so that people can be fully productive; thus enabler can have a managerial meaning.

In the church today, even in the interpretation of scripture, what are the hermeneutic models? Why, therapy and management![48] These days, CEO seems to mean "Church Executive Officer." Now both models, therapy and management, seem to suppose that the congregation per se possesses the Holy Spirit, and therefore needs nothing more than executive cultivation. So in some churches we have a fundamentalist Word of God Bible and a charismatic Holy Spirit-filled congregation and, in between, a preacher best described as "one without authority."[49]

Result: Preaching is no longer a two-edged Word of God. Instead, preaching serves the needs of the church through the voice of an "enabler."[50]

Of course, the shift in the role of preaching may be inevitable. Most mainline denominations are shrinking these days. We are losing membership rapidly.[51] For that matter, so is American Christianity. A "Doonesbury" cartoon a few years ago showed Doonesbury's bearded minister addressing an all but empty church—a tiny huddle of elderly people—saying, "Our day will come again."[52] So every denomination these days seems to be into self-preservation, or better, identity-preservation. Therefore, prophetic preaching is a luxury preachers feel they can't afford, particularly when most mainline Christians appear to be politically conservative. Instead, we read Will Willimon and Stanley Hauerwas, who seem to offer a theological justification for self-preservation.[53] Let's tell *our* story. Let's preserve *our* tradition. Let's hunker down and hold onto ourselves in the name of the Lord. Result: The gospel becomes the gospel of church and "the Word of the Lord is not heard in the land."[54] What is our contention? The two-edged sword—the word of God set over the church and, yes, over the nations—the two-edged sword has been shattered and replaced by safe, solid-looking church logos. At the end of the "Protestant Era," an embattled Protestantism seems to have taken over the Word of God for promotional purposes. And perhaps we must await another Reformation.

When churches are into self-preservation, you would suppose that they would turn to evangelism. Such does not appear to be the case. The literature on preaching in our century has been primarily concerned with preaching biblical texts to faithful in-church people. Perhaps such an emphasis may go all the way back to the Reformers themselves. Almost everything the Reformers wrote on preaching had to do with speaking from the Bible to congregations of believers; as we have noted, they had little missionary interest. But some of the blame must be handed over to Karl Barth.[55] Barth had little interest in any wisdom the world might offer; he had no real wish to engage the world in conversation. His focus was on revelation and faith alone. Such has been the pattern of

American churches during the mid-twentieth century. Except for conservative churches, we have not worried much over apologetic strategies.[56] As a result, there is a peculiar biblical isolation to preaching in the mainline denominations. Is it possible that Barthian biblicism has been a social ploy, a way of holding onto white Protestant identity in a world where rather clearly white Protestants are fast becoming a distinct minority? The Bible emphasizes our evangelical commission; "Go tell," the words command us. We have had departments of evangelism but in large part they are motivated by denominational self-interest. In the religious marketplace, survival is still the name of the game!

On Preaching the Preaching of Christ

So now ask: How can preaching once more be a two-edged sword? How can the pulpit speak words from the mouth of Christ risen? Obviously, we cannot step back in time to rehabilitate a sixteenth-century Protestant mind. Clocks do not spin backward in God's world. Besides, nostalgia, even nostalgia that chases tradition, is never a Christian virtue. So how can the preached word recover proper theological meaning?

A modest suggestion: Let us once more preach the preaching of Christ. According to the Gospel of Mark, "Jesus came to Galilee, proclaiming the good news of God, and saying, 'The time is fulfilled, and the kingdom of God has come near; repent and believe in the good news.'" (Mark 1:14–15) Once more let us announce the coming of God's new order. Have you noticed there seems to be a pendulum swing in the history of preaching? There are times when the gospel seems to be defined by vertical analogy: a human world below and a God world above. In such times, the pulpit tends to elevate Christ himself, saying, repent and believe in Jeeeesus—Jesus being spelled with at least three extra e's! But in other eras vertical analogies have crumbled. They are in-between periods, often gripped by a sense of apocalyptic urgency, and they seem to understand the world horizontally.[57] In such periods, the pulpit stands once more with Christ to proclaim the coming of what Jesus called the

49

basileia tou theou, "kingdom of God": "The time is now, God's new order is at hand; good news, repent, and believe."

Most of us are deeply suspicious of a gospel that even mentions the word "kingdom." Kingdom talk smacks of turn-of-the-century theological liberalism, and we have been taught to steer clear of kingdom-of-God liberalism. Besides, ever since political elections of the late 1980s, people are leery of the "L" word. Nevertheless, in a time of social chaos when any sensitive human being lives in what Frank Kermode terms the "sense of an ending,"[58] now we must once more preach announcing the eschatological notion of God's new social order.

Why? Why would we preach a social vision? Well, because the preaching of God's new order could undercut the nostalgic triumphalism that seems to be rife in American churches. As we all know, John Calvin had a high doctrine of the church as the body of Christ. What kept his understanding of church honest? Answer: Eschatology. In Calvin's thought, there are no earthly ultimates, only ambiguities. Remember what the first letter of T-U-L-I-P signifies? Total depravity. No, if salvation is eschatological fulfillment, then here and now triumphalism is always suspect. If we are a body of Christ, and we are, the term is not to be understood triumphantly; we are emphatically *not* Christ. No, our union with Christ is always a union of sinners and savior.

So at present the body of Christ is deformed and unlovely, and is dignified only by Christ our head; his Word and Spirit give us life. If we preach God's new order, what Jesus called the kingdom, a world in which there is no more war (and no more patriotism!), or racism, or sexism, or denominationalism for that matter, a world in which God's law is scribbled on the heart and love abounds; then by contrast we will mark the fierce fallibilities of our land and our churches.

In America these days, the mainline churches seem to have been driven crazy by membership loss; they are badly frightened. "The Reformed tradition," we cry with the same desperation as fading actors shout, "the show must go on." But all our traditions are called in question by news of God's new order. "New World-a-Coming," wrote the great African-American leader Roi Ottley; it is our gospel as well.[59]

News of the kingdom of God, of course, can restore an evangelical impulse to our churches. "Go tell"; the command is still our mandate. But evangelism has been trapped of late between church-growth hype and the psychological personalism of "relationship-with-Jesus" preaching, neither of which is terribly appealing. The one produces "full-service/production-number" churches and the other a kind of turned-on sweaty religious adolescence! But think about preaching the coming of God's new order to a disillusioned America, weary of narcissism and nostalgia, hankering for new social vision. The message, "Come to a Presbyterian Church" (or fill in your denominational name) is a singularly unattractive offer, but "Come join the new humanity" is an exciting prospect. Today's culture contains a strange longing for a new beginning. We are not referring to hope of psychological renewal, a kind of Tillichian participation in New Being. No, because what's the good of feeling new inside if we're stuck in a same old world, dominated by corrupted "powers that be." No, the chronic plot in much contemporary fiction is the creation of a new society after some sort of apocalyptic calamity—if only the world could begin all over again, simpler and sweeter.[60] The good news is of God's coming new order disrupting our social stability but promising redemption. Come, come be part of a new humanity transforming God's world; that's the heart of Christian evangelism—*not* church, but kingdom.

Of course, if we preach an eschatological vision, we must not be naive. We must define the gospel we proffer with some theological precision. Can we admit that turn-of-the-century theological liberalism was astonishingly naive? We can sing along with children the sweet visionary song, "We're Building a City," but we had better keep in mind that we are building with corrupt contractors, an inept work force, and an out-of-control management—we are, after all, spectacular sinners! Yes, the vision of God's ultimate purpose fills Bible pages, from beginning to end. God's world is designed for reconciliation with no disfigurements of racism or sexism or class; a world of *shalom* in which warfare is a past-tense horror, happily forgotten; a world distinguished by God's own brand of passionate justice. Though the vision fills Bible pages, actual

51

blueprints seem unavailable, and the earthly funding is nil. Thus, in the last pages of the Bible, the Holy City is depicted coming down (present tense!) out of heaven. Nevertheless, God's promises are sure. God's dream is not idle fantasy; it *shall be*. If it is God's dream, in a way it already is! The parables, the sharp edgy teachings, the grand Beatitudes, the apocalyptic passion of Paul—all the Christian scriptures seem to suppose that Christ *is* risen and the kingdom *is* inaugurated. Once more the pulpit is called to speak somewhere between hard realism (we are sinners!) and vision (Christ is risen!), announcing God's new humanity on the face of our badly scarred earth.

The Sword That Saves Our Lives

We have argued that in both the scriptures and the Protestant Reformation, preaching is a two-edged sword. Preaching is a word of God to the church. As Word of God, preaching is both judgment and mercy; it harrows and it heals the church. But, as Luther insists, the Word in preaching is always *extra nos*. We do not possess a word of God tucked away in our own psyches or hidden in the spirit (small "s") of our congregations. No, the word of the gospel message is emphatically God's Word—it is *not* a human wisdom, a technology, or a therapeutic insight. If the word is somehow hidden in our humanity, we scarcely need to call upon God; all we have to do is investigate ourselves with a kind of gnostic psychological passion. No. Let us claim our heritage beyond all the encounter groups and spiritual discovery circles: We are sinners and we do not possess a saving word on our own. The Word of God always addresses the church from beyond the church.

But here's the big question: How can we reinstate a notion of God's Word when we have no real sense of the presence of God? We live in a secular age, an age full of aimless longing and alien absence. Of course, we Christians lately have cooperated with the secular world by denying any notion of a general revelation in nature or in human nature. Instead, as church people, we have clutched our Bibles tighter, repeating over and over, "Word of God," "Word of God," like Jeremiah's temple-goers.[61] We seem to suppose that God speaks, not from beyond, but from within, from within Bible-study circles of our churches! No, the pulpit will have to step beyond a rejection of natural theology and once more *invoke* the Mystery, the living mystery of God. Once more we will have to point to the complexities of cosmos and the deep-pool mysteries of self. We will have to invoke the real presence of mystery so that once more God may speak from beyond the lopsided circles of human wisdom. How do we rehabilitate the Word of God *extra nos?* In our pulpits we will stand before mystery and announce the presence of the living God who speaks, whose sharp word can stab us awake. The word of Christ is a two-edged sword that could cauterize the church.

3

Preaching and Culture

A young student drifted into the office some months ago and complained that he served four different congregations. "I perceive you're a Methodist," we remarked. No, it turned out the young man's four congregations were all wrapped up in one. There were the 1950s Christians who couldn't understand why the church wasn't expanding; they wanted more members and bigger buildings. Then there were the 1960s Christians who kept talking about "getting involved." They were followed by 1970s Christians, many of whom were still keeping faith-journey diaries. Mostly, he was stuck with 1980s Christians who, filled with nostalgia, wanted to turn back to old-time religion. "You see," he said plaintively, "I have four congregations!" He is not alone. Here we are in the 1990s, and churches are still haunted by cultural styles from the past. But then, we never preach Christian faith to empty heads; the gospel addresses all sorts of well-formed culture faiths in any congregation. Now, let us consider preaching and culture.[1]

Dramatis Personae for a Theory

We will begin with definitions. What is culture? As every sociologist knows, culture is a vague word.[2] The word is too big to define with any precision. So instead, under the influence of Crane Brinton's great *History of Western Morals*, we will speak of "cultural formulations."[3] By cultural formulation, we mean the beliefs, the common, often tacit assumptions that characterize a particular time and place and people. Take a case in point: Suppose, on a single day, doing your back-periodical reading in some doctor's office, you scan a popular magazine and find the credo of a Hollywood starlet, "I believe that people are good down deep," she blathers sweetly. Later, leafing paperback pages of *To Kill a Mockingbird*, which oddly enough is in the same office, you come across a final scene in which the young girl, Scout, says of someone, "Atticus, he was real nice . . . ," and her father, Atticus Finch, replies, "Most people are, Scout, when you finally see them."[4] Then, in a back-issue news magazine, you read an article quoting a noted Harvard expert on penal reform who supposes that proper sentencing will permit prisoners to blossom and to realize innate virtues. You might gather all the statements together and suppose that twentieth-century Americans tend to affirm the innate goodness of human nature—one little strand in an intricate pattern of belief. Cultural formulations are made up of many such strands. Though cultures are complex, they are distinguishable: Can we not talk of the Renaissance? Or mention an Elizabethan mind? Or refer to late-nineteenth-century Romanticism, and know what we mean? We are referring to style, to conventions of speech and behavior, to social attitudes, and above all to shared assumptions. So much by way of introduction to the notion of a cultural formulation.

The other term of our discussion is more difficult to define: Christian faith. Has anyone successfully delineated an "essence of Christianity?"[5] When you stretch Christianity across the centuries, obviously it changes. We teach courses in the history of doctrine because the shape of our faith has been revised again and again. Christian faith has translated itself into many tongues and has dallied with many philosophies. Will the real Christian faith please stand up!

Even if we go back to biblical sources, we discover that early Christian literature is varied.[6] Can we reconcile the apocalyptic Gospel of Mark with the later letters to Timothy?

Not easily. No wonder that good Catholics giggle when they hear that famous episcopal phrase, "The church has always and everywhere taught that . . . ". They know perfectly well that the church has never "always and everywhere" taught anything with too much consistency. Where can we find an essential Christianity? Can we sum up faith as the love commandment? No, according to Denis de Rougement, love is differently depicted from age to age—even by the church.[7] Or should we insist that Christianity is nothing more or less than Christ, his life and death and resurrection? No, all you have to do is to study Christ's different depictions down through the ages—a warrior, a king, a mystic, a knight, a nineteenth-century aesthete, and goodness knows what else.[8] Christian faith is always embodied; it's wrapped up in different cultural packages. So, an "essence of Christianity" is mighty hard to come by.

Nevertheless, Christians in every age are aware of their faith. Moreover, they recognize their faith by contrast with the ethos of their culture. For example, do we not paste labels on ourselves? We are both Christian and American. Certainly, no one would wish to put an equal sign between the two terms. Even twentieth-century Americans can sense an intrinsic difference between an adulation of National Football League power and Jesus Christ hung up to die—winning is apparently not everything in God's world! So, standing in the mind of our age, we can view our faith as different and perhaps even as peculiar. Alternately, standing in faith we can regard the values, attitudes, and desires of the worldly world as somewhat alien. Do we not experience a degree of Sunday dismay with regard to our Monday-through-Saturday patterns of life? So, though it is almost impossible to define essential Christianity, we can recognize the terms of our discussion; we sense in ourselves a difference. Thus we will speak of Christian faith and of cultural formulations. So much for our dramatis personae; the one a faith and the other a cultural formation.

Moving in on Culture

There are times when faith moves into culture evangelically. Look at the first century: Early Christian expansion involved moving into a Greco-Roman world. At the outset, Christianity was essentially a Jewish sect. Yet, even in scripture, Christian faith is moving out from itself toward a different cultural milieu.[9] Supposedly, the book of Acts records the beginning of the shift from Jewish sect to a Gentile mission.[10] So let us ask: How does Christian faith move into a different cultural formulation?

Obviously, a first step is translation. Though Martin Hengel is no doubt right in arguing that early Christians were probably bilingual,[11] nonetheless the Jewishness of Christianity had to be transferred to a Greek mind. Translation is, of course, much more than a matter of x = y, a word for a word.[12] As we all know, words are ideas; they are ways of thinking. Some years ago, a Bible translator told of an African tongue without an equivalent word for "faith." What translators did was to grab a word used to describe a warrior flinging himself down in a hammock to rest after battle.[13] Thus, the translation encouraged a somewhat Lutheran understanding of faith as justified passivity. Eugene Nida provides still another case:

> In Nilotic Shilluk, for example, the only way one can talk about God's forgiveness is literally, "God spit on the ground in front of us." This idiom arises from the practice of plaintiffs and defendants having to spit on the ground in front of each other when finally a case has been tried and punishments have been meted out and fines paid. The spitting (which has an entirely different cultural value from what it has with us) symbolizes that the case is terminated, that all is forgiven, and that the accusations cannot come into court again.[14]

But notice that the metaphor involved is from litigation and therefore the understanding of forgiveness may be tied to a legal model; presumably, sin will be understood as lawbreaking. Doing translation is not a simple act; translation is not trading one word for another. No, the act of translating *changes* faith.

But moving into a different culture is much more than finding new words. Preaching must explain the faith.[15] In explaining, preachers reach for metaphor and simile. They draw analogies saying: "Christian faith is *like* . . . ," and then they describe an image or an idea or an event with which an audience is familiar.[16] Early Christian apologists wielded metaphor and image to express Christian understandings in patterns of Greek thought. Actually, precedent had already been set by Philo, who attempted to relate Judaism to the Greek world: God was *to on*, "Being," Torah was *logos*, Messiah was archetypal man, and Word of God was a divine emanation; x is *like* y.[17] So Christianity, employing a preacher's strategy, extended itself with the word *"like."* Early church leaders employed analogy, yes, and sometimes even allegory,[18] as they tried to explain Christian conviction in alien territory.[19] For an early example, take a look at Paul's speech in Athens.[20] According to Acts, Paul spots a local shrine built for "an unknown god," whom he identifies as the God of Christian community. But he draws a distinction, saying that the true God doesn't live in shrines—an idea often ventured by Greek philosophers. Then he goes on to depict the creation in decidedly Greek terms. Paul even quotes phrases from Greek philosophers and poets, saying, "in him we live and move and have our being" and "we are God's offspring." In preaching, early Christian apologists had to fit one set of ideas into another. In the same way, early Christian artists were apologists when they pictured Moses as a Roman senator or Christ as a young Apollo.[21] Likewise, Christian worshipers borrowed ritual practice and even hymnody from the pagan mysteries.[22] Preaching did much the same thing. The key word was "like," and the tactic was analogy. So, tick off the strategies: translation, analogy, allegory, ritual, art. There are times when, with evangelical enthusiasm, Christian faith moves into a culture.

Can We Be Co-opted?

Before we go further, let's stop and face a problem. Is there a hidden danger in evangelism? Missionary strategy tends to render faith palatable; can faith become too palatable? Could we ever end up with an equal sign between Christianity and a cultural formulation? Might the faith once declared by prophets and apostles be absorbed into culture and virtually disappear? For example, look at what happened to Christianity under the aegis of Enlightenment? Crane Brinton suggests a pattern of change.[23] The theological categories of Law vs. Grace became Civilization vs. the Natural Self—as represented by the gamey gamekeeper in *Lady Chatterley's Lover*[24] or by Paul Gauguin's ripe native girls; the Second Coming turned into Utopia; original sin became environmental corruption or, sometimes, after Darwin, an evolutionary lag; God's covenant turned into natural law; eternal life was reduced to eternal values; and providence gave way to Hegel's historical dialectic. The recital may seem extreme, but study the popular preaching of the period and you discover how easily Christian faith was crowded into a particular cultural formulation. It happens. In some American pulpits these days, has our faith been turned into right-wing politics or a pulpit edition of *Psychology Today*? Sense the danger and ask the question: Can Christian faith be fully translated into a culture faith?

Answer: Maybe, but maybe not. There always seem to be areas of tension, ideas in Christian faith that resist analogy. Always there is what Emil Brunner called the scandal of Christianity,[25] namely, the aporia of the cross. Christianity is news of God disclosed in the impotent foolishness of the cross, a God of love who is willing to die in a thoroughly ungodly way for the sake of humanity. Culturally, we long for a different sort of God, a God for "The Hour of Power," a do-all, cure-all God, who is adjunct to our needs or, better, our desires or, still better, our prides. But see the figure of Jesus Christ: He was arrested, condemned, tossed in jail, sentenced to death, roughed up by soldiers, made a public spectacle, and finally done in by an unusually cruel form of capital punishment. Christian faith has the outright gall to point to the figure of Jesus, a disgraced loser, and say, "There is our God!" Is there any way the message of the cross will ever be culturally palatable? No wonder faith spreads rapidly with those who are judged, deprived, condemned, or oppressed. Otherwise, to be truthful, Christian faith is a hard sell, isn't it? Maybe we need not worry, because at core the Christian message is tough to assimilate. Will the scandal of the cross ever jibe with any cultural formulation?

Other areas of tension have been chronic. In every age they seem to prevent the assimilation of Christian faith by some cultural formulation. Look at the biblical notion of creation. According to the Judeo-Christian tradition, God created all things and then pronounced them very good.[26] Oddly enough, the notion that the physical world, its crass animal character as well as its sensuous beauty, is essentially good is not a popular idea. Most cultural formulations seem to endorse a Manichean split, a disdain for mundane matter, a lesser label for the earth's earthiness. Again and again, a kind of gnostic pride seems to emerge in cultural formulations—mind over matter, spirit over flesh. So when cheerful Christians show up enjoying the good stuff of earth like partying pagans, the world is usually appalled! No, a true religion must be of a higher, wiser, purer nature than such pleasure-taking believers display. Actually prim Christians, who have confused culture religion with Christianity, are often as offended; they too hanker after a spirituality spelled with extra "r"s—"spirrrrrrituality," and are deeply suspicious of the earth's "lower" order of physical things.[27] So, mark a Christian doctrine of creation; it usually troubles exponents of culture religion.

Then there's the resurrection. Remember how Paul's address at Athens was going so well until he made a tactical blunder and mentioned the resurrection of Jesus (Acts 17:30–32):

> "While God has overlooked the times of human ignorance, now he commands all people everywhere to repent, because he has fixed a day on which he will have the world judged in righteousness by a man whom he has appointed, and of this he has given assurance to all by raising him from the dead." When they heard of the resurrection of the dead, some scoffed; but others said, "We will hear you again about this."

Most developed cultures are built on analogy; they live in the midst of a two-way-mirror system of correspondence. All great eras seem to have embraced notions of correspondence. The neo-Platonists revered a higher realm of "forms"; and, although our world was no more than a flickering shadow of reality in encaved darkness, nevertheless there was some correspondence: ". . . now we see in a mirror, dimly." Surely in the high medieval period, people affirmed hierarchies of heaven reflected in the hierarchies of earth.[28] Then in the eighteenth century there was a notion of divine rationality in nature reflecting in the divine reason of human beings.[29] Ideas of correspondence encourage intimations of immortality. If something is out there, or up there, like us, then surely we can anticipate eternal extension. Eugène Ionesco captures the mood when he has his "hero," Bérenger, elated in a world of utopian Idealism:

> "Gardens, blue sky, or the spring which corresponds to the universe inside . . . or a mirror in which its own smile could be reflected . . . a smiling being in a smiling world . . . I felt I could go on living, and yet I couldn't die."[30]

But Christian faith begins with the book of Job's blunt answer, "No," to the question, "If mortals die, will they live again?"[31] We are mortal and we die—"all flesh is grass." Yet, at the same time, Christians announce the resurrection of Jesus Christ. To make matters worse, Christians stand up and chant a creed that includes the peculiar phrase, "resurrection of the body."[32] So, in effect, our faith denies proud claims of permanence—we are *not* by nature immortal—and, at the same time, hands out an utterly incredible, fairy-tale notion of resurrection. So the gospel doesn't fit into most cultural formulations. Happily, there are always troubling points of tension.

On Getting Out in Time

There are other times when faith pulls away. When tension between faith and culture enlarges, then faith must turn against itself—that is, against its own cultural expression. Though the alliance of Reformation Christianity and Enlightenment was productive, the synthesis is now in disarray. Perhaps the alliance was shattered by the subjective–objective split, a split between reason and romanticism, because in America these days we have both a pseudorational fundamentalism and a charismatic "heart" religion. Did the descriptive natural sciences undercut Christian natural theology and then Freud sabotage the inner testimony of the Spirit? Perhaps twentieth-century neo-orthodoxy must be viewed as a return to origins amid a tough era of intellectual assault. More likely, the rationalism of the Enlightenment was in obvious self-destruct, and Christianity was getting out from under while the getting was good! In any event, American Christianity is now sadly divided between conservative churches desperately trying to hold on to a previous Christian synthesis and more liberal churches simply seeking to secure their own social status. And yet, what is needed is theological reconstruction amid the shambles of a collapsed ("Henny Penny, the sky *has* fallen!") cultural formulation.

How does Christianity withdraw faith from crumbling cultural alliances? The strategy is basically a matter of reversal. First, if something called modernity seems to have corrupted faith, then you take a backward turn. So the Christian community returns to sources, namely, to the Bible and/or early church tradition, obduring all philosophical entanglements. The biblical theology movement sought to rehabilitate what was supposed to be an original, uniquely biblical way of thinking and as a result was downright hostile to all forms of philosophical theology. Second, if you have aligned with culture through translation, then, to exit, you will promote a return to original languages. Exegetical word study will become vogue; perhaps you may even publish a multivolume work on biblical words such as Gerhard Kittel's remarkable "word-book"![33] Third, if analogy is a missionary strategy, then you deny "likeness," and instead affirm the *sui generis* character of biblical faith. From the start, you will insist, biblical faith was different; it was different from the Semitic world around Israel and, in its Christian form, was different from pagan cultures and Greek philosophies—biblical faith was and is unique! Fourth, you will be eager to deny *analogia entis*, insisting that God is transcendent otherness. Thus, you will reject understandings of *imago Dei* that liken human being to the Being of God.[34] You may sense that cultural syntheses feature notions of correspondence and indeed offer meaning to life by means of such correlations. So you will cancel any notion of general revelation—God cannot be known in nature or human experience—and insist that God is revealed only in singular events, which happily are scribbled in something called a Bible which, even more happily, we Christians possess. Fifth, if during missionary enterprise you used representational art to picture Jesus in contemporary settings, when you pull away, you must show a distinct preference for nonrepresentational art. You will become a biblical iconoclast. And, sixth, if you borrowed hymns and ritual from indigenous folk religion, when withdrawing from an alliance with culture you will sharply distinguish Christian faith from the trappings of mere religion. What do you do when withdrawing from a culture? Why, you become a Karl Barth! In the twentieth century, Protestant Christianity's dialectical theology can be viewed as a strategy for cultural disengagement.

On Dividing Cultural History

Here is a question: How do you divvy up culture? Most cultural historians will speak of phases. Some phases are obvious: Certainly there are cultural highs, times such as the high medieval years, or perhaps late eighteenth century, which might be termed the height of Enlightenment. From our standpoint, such high periods usually involve a developed synthesis between a cultural formulation and Christian faith. But equally obvious are the lows. They are transitional times such as the breakdown of the Greco-Roman world or the collapse of the medieval synthesis or, obviously, now. Such highs and lows are evident even to untutored historians; the in-between periods may require more subtle analysis. Of course, there is a proper resistance to the whole notion of phases in human history, particularly among historians, a cautious crowd, who quite rightly fear reading value judgments into the human story. But reading the human story one way or another is inevitable.[35] Is there some objective perch outside of history for scientific historians? No, human beings come equipped with memory, brooding, and hope, and thus with story-shaped minds. To read some kind of plot into chronological events is to be human. So we will take the risk.[36]

Now let's spin the world and see where we are. Almost anyone who pokes at cultural history sees phases, epochal phases in Western cultural history. Perhaps if we knew enough, we could trace patterns in African cultural history—a task yet to be fulfilled.[37] But if we are looking at Christian faith in its cultural development, we are probably looking at a Greco-Roman world, a medieval world, and what we have come to call the Enlightenment.[38] In each of these epochal moments, we can discern similar phases. We are not suggesting that history unfolds in recurring cycles. Yes, there is repetition; civilizations rise and fall, again and again. But as Arnold Toynbee observed long ago, though events recur like the turning of a wheel, in Christian history the wheel is headed somewhere; history is teleologically conceived.[39] Christianity anticipates denouement. In other words, the meaning of history is ultimately eschatological. Meanwhile, let's look at some recurring patterns in the checkered, somewhat indecent relationship between Christian faith and cultural formulations.

Cultures Taking Shape

When Christian faith begins to form within a culture, it seeds itself in disparate strands of thought and subcultural communities so that, as the culture comes together, Christian faith will be there. Of course, in times of cultural change, there may be a leftover, establishment Christianity as well. In transitional times, the religious community can be sharply divided.[40] Nevertheless, Christian faith spreads rapidly, *re-forming* itself among the poor and disenfranchised.[41] Thus in our day we are astonished by Christianity multiplying all over Africa, Asia, and in sprawling ghettos of South America.[42] Simultaneously, an established, fairly affluent Christian community appears to be shrinking in America and much of Europe. When faith moves into a newly developing culture, faith aligns with countercultural people. Christianity enters culture by spreading subculturally.[43]

Formative periods are marked by a highly metaphorical, expanding language. The culture is coining new words; in a way, the culture is renaming the world. New language is formed orally. It is fashioned in subcultural linguistic ghettos as well as by interaction with other languages that previously may have been marginalized. For example, American English, which had been shrinking, is now enlarging as it picks up new words from ghettoized African-American and Spanish-speaking subcultures as well as from other languages—as Korean immigrants increase, for example, churches will soon learn to name concepts such as "Han" and "Minjung theology."[44] Of course, language is primarily renewed by metaphor. While established language has metaphor, images have usually become stock, or even trite—for instance, "Time is money."[45] Language is renewed as new metaphors bring out previously unconsidered experience. And, with the forming of new language, the world is renewed.

Frequently, periods of change are characterized by what might be termed epistemological shifts, changes in the way in which people *think* as they use language. Within Western cultural history, such alterations in consciousness have been a shift from speaking to writing,[46] a shift from writing to printing,[47] and now a shift involving electronic symbols and procedures. In eras when faith moves into a culture, language is orally formed, metaphorical, and expanding. Linguistic expansion is often accelerated by new modes of communication.

Oddly enough, tragedies seem to be written in formative eras—Greek tragedy, Shakespearean tragedy and perhaps, during medieval years, the tragic, staged drama of the Mass. Tragic theater tends to establish the "gods" above, a structure of myth, meaning, and custom that Peter Berger calls the "sacred canopy."[48] Put yourself into an audience watching a tragedy. If you are viewing a well-written play, you will identify with the tragic hero or heroine; you will feel with them. In some way or another, tragic heroes always defy the culture's "gods"— Orestes becomes involved in a forbidden dalliance or Hamlet presumptuously takes vengeance into his own hands.[49] Thus, when the tragic hero or heroine is killed off, something in us may also perish. But, please note, life goes on, and the culture "gods" are vindicated; they are even more firmly established. Thus, tragedy helps to construct and affirm the culture's sacred canopy. No wonder tragedies tend to be written during times of cultural formation.

As Christianity moves into a forming culture, there is often a venturesome theologian, a person such as Augustine or Luther, who will move out of a contrapuntal posture and constructively reformulate the faith in very new ways. Because neo-orthodoxy is basically a conservative movement—it is neo-Reformation in its Protestant expression—neo-orthodoxy is not capable of reformulating faith for a new age. Clearly, Augustine set his stamp on centuries of medieval thought just as Luther and John Calvin determined basic patterns of Protestant thought for more than four hundred years. Such formative theologians rather deliberately align themselves with emerging philosophies and reconceptualize Christianity for a new cultural epoch. We are not referring to what David Tracy has labeled a "revisionist" position.[50] Philosophical theologians in formative periods correlate with emerging strands of thought so that, as a cultural formulation begins to be defined, theological patterns of meaning will be available.

During formative periods, preaching speaks freely in popular language, language close to everyday speech, and reaches out in search of analogies to explain traditional Christian doctrine in a new way. Thus, though there may be biblical metaphors for atonement—sacrifice, ransom, victory in battle—such traditional images may no longer communicate effectively. Yes, terrorism and ransomed prisoners are still front-page news, but animal sacrifice is seldom practiced in local United Methodist churches, and images of warfare probably have been corrupted by the high-tech Pentagon. Anselm's notion of "satisfaction" as well as "judicial" metaphors from the Reformation period may be equally passé. So, as a cultural formation begins to come together, preachers must seek new, "two-way" metaphor; metaphor to convey God's mysterious grace and, at the same time, human experiences of sin and liberation. Christian preaching must play

on "the edges of language" where metaphor brings out redefi-
nitions of human experience.[51] To quote Wallace Stevens:

> Throw away the lights, the definitions,
> And say what you see in the dark
>
> That it is this or that it is that,
> But do not use *the rotted names*.[52]

Preaching is Christian faith explaining itself anew with imagination and precision—"That it is this or that it is that"—beyond the rotten slogans and leftover clichés from a previous
age.[53] If preachers do speak from scripture, pulpit hermeneutic will tend to be broad, favoring Alexandria rather than An-
tioch, so as to venture apologetic analogies.

Homiletic form is usually experimental, because preachers are developing rhetoric to match the shape of a new,
forming human consciousness.[54] Human consciousness
changes with history, and such changes appear to be
epochal. Thus in every new era rhetoric will be reconsidered.
During much of the twentieth century, with homiletics
under the sway of biblical theology, rhetoric has been regarded with suspicion as a form of alien human wisdom. Instead, many homiletic books have tried to derive method
from the Bible alone. But in every formative period there is a
developing new rhetoric.[55] People hear and understand in
very different ways, and useful rhetoric tries to match speaking and hearing. We can learn to shape the language of
speaking so that people will more readily grasp meaning
and believe. Remember the apostle Paul's flat-out homiletic
fact of life: "Faith comes from hearing!"

Riding High

What about the high periods? What about eras of synthesis
in which Christian faith and a cultural formulation have come
together. These are happy times when most people everywhere share a common worldview. Like tadpoles in a pond,

they cannot conceive of any other worlds of meaning. There's something "set" about the culture in high periods. The age "understands" and is busy spreading its understanding to all phases of life. Thus, etiquette books can be written because conduct has accepted conventions and dictionaries can be compiled because language is well-defined for everyone to learn. In the highs, cultures may tend to celebrate themselves with baroque art and defined architectural display. In such eras, we can recognize a "style"—for example, the vaulted gothic of the medieval synthesis. Even theology seems to have taken shape; theological manuals for believers can be written in high periods. Again, there is a tendency to expand the synthesis achieved between theology and the cultural formulation so that a "christendom" may be established.

On stage are comedies. Yes, other dramatic forms are always available in every age, but during cultural high periods the major dramatic form is comedy and, often comedy of manners. Comic heroes don't have to be killed off like tragic figures; after all, they'll come around. Comedy's message is social adjustment and social reward. So the happy ending to a comedy usually includes social status, financial security, and the sweet domestications of marriage. When you view comedy, you identify with characters who often skirt dire dangers or even teeter on the edge of rebellion. But then characters accommodate themselves, and social order is preserved. If tragedy affirms a sacred canopy, comedy affirms a less transcendent social order. Basically a "happy ending" is happy because inwardly audiences approve of social adjustment. Some scholars argue that, in view of resurrection, Christian faith must be considered "comedic," but we demur.[56] No, the eschatological message of a coming "kingdom" is scarcely an endorsement of social status quo. But then we do not hear much kingdom preaching during the high periods, unless the kingdom is preached as expanding christendom.

High periods are vertical. All high periods seem to look up; they seem to be convinced that there is something up there or out there like us. Remember the hierarchies of heaven to match hierarchies on earth, a rational deity related to human reason, or the eternal forms casting shadows on our encaved lives? Therefore, in the vertically oriented high periods, prayer life comes easy!

Preaching is fairly stereotyped during high periods; it has a method. Usually, a rhetoric/homiletic has been defined earlier—for example, Augustine's *De doctrina Christiana*,[57] which determined the course of medieval rhetoric—but during the high periods patterns are elaborated and firm rules of rhetoric are established. After all, the high periods have a stable vocabulary and common speech conventions. Again, at the time of the Renaissance, rhetoric was renewed by scholars such as Erasmus—in homiletics, Luther must be cited—but later, English rhetoric was elaborated by the likes of Hugh Blair and Richard Whately.[58] Sermons during the high periods are carefully designed and often feature the same illustrations, illustrations that are stock understandings of particular Christian convictions. Thus, preaching in the high periods is quite good but is scarcely innovative theologically.

Tumbling Towers of Babel

Like towers of Babel, cultural syntheses can come tumbling down. Perhaps, they become oppressively static. Cultural highs are triumphant periods, defined vertically by some notion of correspondence. Thus, they are threatened by horizontal movement—that is, by the journeying course of history. Is it any wonder that Frederick Hoffman can argue that periods of cultural collapse are preoccupied with death and history.[59] From the standpoint of Christian faith, though churches may prosper during high periods, we still pray that God's "will be done." For the one-way movement of history is instigated by God's will and moves toward a fulfillment of God's good purpose. Thus, any attempt to live in vertical stasis forever, enjoying vertical pieties under an elaborately woven sacred canopy, can be a form of cultural idolatry. The phrase "tower of Babel" is well chosen. Perhaps the social edifice of high, synthetic epochs, though bright with human achievement and filled with a fine religious awareness, is, after all, hubris. Does the idolatrous character of a high period seek to preserve its permanence against the sweeping tides of time? Perhaps. Cultural highs can become coercive and breed countercultural opposition so that eventually the towers crumble.

On the dramatic stage, times of cultural dissolution usually are accompanied by an increase in both farce and melodrama. In a way, they are both corruptions of classical form, comedy and tragedy. In farce, the comic hero, society's child, has become a victim. Social conventions are oppressive or even absurd, constricting human life. Thus, farcical heroes or heroines are culturally impudent. Like Charlie Chaplin's insightful tramp, they will show up the oppressions of surrounding culture or, like Keystone Kops, will lampoon social forces of law and order. Nevertheless, farcical heroes lose out. In the end, they are banished. Did Chaplin's tramp have a permanent home? They get the custard pie-in-the-face treatment, or their neckties are snipped, or as in Greek farce, they are knocked flat on their faces. We, the audience, howl with laughter. But though we cheer on impudence, with laughter we accept our own terrible captivity; the social order must still be preserved.

Melodrama may also be viewed as a corruption, a corruption of the tragic. The "gods" or "demons" of tragedy seem to impinge on the world of melodrama but as lesser ghosts, small-scale terrors, or shivery threats of death.[60] But, in the end, all threats are exorcised or turn out to be imaginary; social chaos is averted and we return to our everyday reality. In melodrama, passé conventional "gods" may be conventionally affirmed, but they have no reality and no awesomeness. Melodrama may excite us but at the cost of faith. For melodrama is actually a cynical form of drama.

Preaching suffers during times of breakdown, because not only has language become impoverished but also traditional rhetorical conventions no longer hold true. Language actually shrinks, our social vocabulary gets smaller, and words become somewhat abstracted—what Philip Wheelwright terms "block language."[61] Words are still a medium of exchange, but they are losing connection with lived experience; perhaps "vacuity" best describes the language. A recent work analyzing contemporary language is appropriately entitled, *The B.S. Factor: The Theory and Technique of Faking It in America.*[62] Contemporary preaching seems to speak a minimal, common-denominator language, language spoken in the well-lit busy center of life; our preaching language fills time and offers easy insight, but seems incapable of invoking any real presence of God. Our language contains little metaphor, and the subtle evocative precisions of the poet are largely absent. We may communicate, but we no longer seem to reveal. Except for the great preachers of the black pulpit, homiletic method has been reduced. If you examine homiletic texts used in the middle fifty years of our century, for the most part they are abbreviated "how-to" books compared to the substantial rhetorical homiletics published by Alexandre Vinet, John A. Broadus, and others in the nineteenth century.[63] The sermons we preach are shorter and less demanding of listeners; we seem to be busy these days producing little Bible homilies. In times of cultural breakdown, traditional rhetorical wisdom is no longer wise; that is, rhetoric no longer relates to how human beings actually hear and grasp meaning.

At the nadir of cultural collapse, when the two-way mirror of correspondence has been shattered, we are apt to get both a "death of God" theology[64] and an indistinct image of humanity—think of Henry Moore's sculptured figures, hollowed out, soulless, with holes where their hearts should be.[65] We live in a kind of inverse cultural correspondence or, better, absence. At the nadir, perhaps our style is irony, a theater of the absurd.[66] Tragic heroes will discover there is no God,[67] and comic figures will decide that society is not worth accommodation.[68] In melodrama, the supernatural will suddenly turn terribly real and our farcical heroes—exiled, custard-pied, knocked down and out—may turn out to be our unsuspected saviors. Perhaps.

So much for a descriptive sketch of cultural phases—enough indeed to offend any competent historian!

Now Where Are We?

Does anyone doubt that we live "between the times?"[69] Can anyone not believe that Western culture is in transition?

71

The phrase "cultural breakdown" describes our era. There is political evidence: Third- and fourth-world peoples are rising while the power of Western nations is, despite American disclaimers, obviously ebbing. Not only that, but suppressed peoples in Western societies are beginning to speak out. Talk of pluralism nowadays recognizes that subcultures and social movements in our own nation are moving from oppressed powerlessness to power. Linguistically, we have lost half a language and are now in the process of having to develop a whole new vocabulary. Thus, we've published dictionaries and translated liturgy and now are doing so all over again. Dwight Macdonald contends that in the 1940s and 1950s language was shrinking, but that since the 1960s, language has begun to expand again.[70] Of course, when language changes in every major tongue on earth, then a whole world is in process of changing its mind. To be blunt, what we have called the Protestant Era, a synthesis of faith and Enlightenment, is over. Just as years ago a Catholic medieval synthesis collapsed, now the four-hundred-year-old Protestant synthesis has fragmented. As a result, we Protestants are defensive; we are desperately trying to hold onto our social position. American churches are pathologically into self-preservation, even though such survival strategies will be ineffective. We are in the midst of cultural change, a change that obviously will not be stayed. To echo Karl Barth's phrase once more, we live "between the times."

So how do we preach? What is the task of homiletics now? We must still separate Christianity from an earlier synthesis. We must separate ourselves from a cultural formulation now in disarray. To do so, the pulpit must be culturally critical. Instead of Barth's turn from culture in the name of an imperious biblicism, we must be willing to take on cultural assumptions that are no longer viable: our blind faith in technological progress,[71] our reliance on the power of death[72]—Is the Pentagon our national monument?—the all-pervasive "triumph of the therapeutic,"[73] and other cultural idols. Not since the 1930s and 1940s has the pulpit truly engaged the cultural mind. But, here's the catch, we must take on ourselves as well. We must speak contrapuntally against an earlier synthetic

Christianity that was grounded in rationalism and pietism and, yes, historicism. To borrow a term from Robert Jenson, we must be "a religion against itself."[74] For such a task, Barth's radical dialectic theology can be useful. Between the ages, preaching must still be committed to cultural disengagement.

Yet, must we not be as much concerned with what might be termed reengagement? Like it or not, we are moving toward a new evangelical enterprise. Somehow, Christian faith must seed itself in countercultural movements that will someday come together to form a new social mind. Once more we are called on to translate ourselves into the thought forms and images of a forming new age. Of course, we mainline types may not be major players; we may be too culturally compromised to be useful. Mainline churches are, after all, establishment, and establishment people do not readily preach good news to the poor! Moreover, they seldom are in touch with anything countercultural. So the task probably will be done for us by Christians in other lands, although the African-American church in America will surely be heard as well as voices from the barrios. Christian faith must engage culture evangelically. We must help the frightened to march, like Jeremiah's exiles, from a collapsed cultural mind into temporary exile. And somehow we must let go of ourselves enough to invest in countercultural peoples who will be the force of the future, the consensus of a new world age. We must seed faith now in the troubled, transitional soil of culture.

Of course, remember that when you move into a new cultural formulation, the first task is a kind of translation. Perhaps the great calling of homiletics these days is the rearticulation of our faith. Has there been a course in apologetics offered by homiletic departments anywhere save in conservative seminaries? Once more, we must be concerned to reformulate Christian faith, to find new metaphors and analogies to explain the gospel message. For fifty years, homiletics has been an adjunct to the biblical theology movement. Now preaching must turn toward a more natural alliance; we must enter into conversation with philosophical theology. Just as philosophy and rhetoric go hand in hand, so properly do philosophical theology and homiletics. When we preach atonement, as of course we must, can we still trot out worn judicial metaphors from the Reformation era? And, in an age of triumphant militarism, dare we risk an unmodified *Christus Victor* model?[75] Homiletics must participate in the recasting of theology. Yes, there are voices in the church today that urge the preservation of our faith story as the number-one task of the churches. But what do we preserve? Enlightenment Christianity has already crumbled. No, once more we must risk faith's conversation with culture. Sometimes, it is called evangelism.

Strategies

Can we draw thoughts together? Can we discern some strategy for the church in the world? Long ago, H. Richard Niebuhr, in his classic work, *Christ and Culture*,[76] spoke of Christ against Culture, Christ of Culture, Christ above Culture, and Christ and Culture in Paradox. Niebuhr's great work, written in 1951, has informed more than forty years of churchly strategy. But today Niebuhr's categories somehow don't quite seem to apply. Perhaps his definition of culture was too static, while our world is frayed in scattered transitional strands. But the issues Niebuhr raised are still with us, and perhaps more so in a time of change.

Do we view culture as a kind of encroaching dark ages in which faithful Christians must seek to preserve their Christian identity? Or is culture a product of human ambiguity—both a sign of our sinfulness and yet strangely a witness to the blessing of humanity by God? What is the church's stance toward culture? We can no longer live in the world chanting Karl Barth's emphatic "Nein," at least not in the 1990s.[77] No, we must think ourselves through to a somewhat different position.

Earlier in these chapters, we suggested that the church's commission is twofold. We are commanded to go into the world with the gospel, the good news of God's new order. At the same time, we are to be a sign, perhaps a sacramental sign of God's new age in an old-order world; we are to display the shape of new creation in our common life. Thus, the church in culture is always torn. On the one hand, we must reach out culturally if we are to preach the gospel. On the other hand, we are to distinguish ourselves from the culture to display some sign of God's new age. One impulse can be world-relating, the other world-rejecting. Of course there's a logic behind our paradoxical commission—a logic found in the cross. The cross convicts the age, every age, and all humanity by exposing our structures of sin. At the same time, we know the cross is a great gesture of God's love toward the world. Love cuts two ways. The church in its common life must be different, rejecting worldly ways that conflict with love; at the same time, the church must reach out in love, offering God to a wearied world. Perhaps, just perhaps, God's love is a clue.

A footnote: How can we preserve the integrity of our Christian faith against the world? Where is the essence of Christianity we are supposed to preserve? Always the gospel is preached in brokenness; always it is distorted. There is no pure gospel; no, not even in the Bible! To be blunt, the Christian scriptures are both sexist and anti-Semitic.[78] Faith is ever an admixture with cultural notions. Perhaps all we can do is to preach at the point of our conversion from the mind of the age, and leave the rest to the working of God's Spirit. But then, that's what preachers have done for centuries. And, the faith has been passed along. Now, once again our job is passing faith along. Like Isaiah, we have stained lips in a sinful world. Thus, our gospel is no doubt tainted. But, nonetheless, from stained lips, the message—God's great love for the world—is saving good news.

4

Preaching and Method

Some years ago the satiric review *Beyond the Fringe*[1] was a smash hit in London, and, a year later, opened on Broadway. The review featured the spoof of a typical Anglican sermon. The text was a single verse from Genesis: "But my brother Esau is an hairy man, but I am a smooth man." The homily began with the text, moved along by whim and association through one pulpit cliché after another and concluded minutes later, with a ringing repetition of the text, every word weighted with significance; "But my brother Esau is an hairy man." A bishop visiting the States was asked for his reaction. "I laughed," he said, "but not loudly." "The satire," he added, was too close to the mark." The bishop was not merely indicting the Anglican pulpit, but was bemoaning Protestant preaching in general. If pulpit conventions can be satirized with ease, then clearly it is time to examine our procedures. Is there any way, any new way to preach that will speak God's good news to our word-weary age? What can we do about homiletic method?

Burden of the Lord

Anyone who preaches regularly wants a method. Indeed, most of us need method simply to survive. The average preacher produces the equivalent of a book a year in sermons; a daunting task, week after week, month after month, year after year. Therefore, however freewheeling ministers may be, they soon embrace a methodical discipline, if only in self-defense. Preachers need a way of preaching that will get the job done faithfully, without hair tugging, endless rewriting, and sweaty last-minute desperations. Of course, we know that method can stifle. Method can turn into an every-week repetitive formula that congregations soon pick up, if only subliminally. Like Erle Stanley Gardner detective stories, if you've heard one sermon, you've heard them all! No, we need a method that marshals our time and energy but sets us free from enacting ourselves psychologically on a weekly basis.[2] After all, our lives are already crowded with parish busyness and the tears of the brokenhearted. There are never enough hours in a day for the work of the Lord. So preachers need method—some sure, sensible way of doing sermons.

Yes, all of us wish for a quick and easy way of preparing sermons. But, if you crowd us into a corner, maybe we will admit the truth; we would like to be able to prepare not just quick sermons, but *good* sermons, sermons that reach deep into the lives of our people and are useful. We know that in preaching, we ought to love our neighbors—rather specifically, our neighbors in the pews. Moreover, we know we ought to love God. What makes slapdash, hasty sermons intolerable is that they are a sure sign of unbelief. If we truly believe that we preach in the presence of God, how can we ever let ourselves be careless? Surely one of the purposes of preaching is invocation. Our sermons should be fit offerings to God in whose awesome presence we dare stand to speak. So, yes, we'd like a quick and easy way of preaching, but more deeply we want our sermons to be worthy of God and useful to our neighbors. So please, in our harried parishes, how do we prepare ourselves to preach and to preach well? Give us responsible method.

Method and Consciousness

The problem of method is now more complex than we know. Human consciousness is historical. Consciousness is

not fixed, the same in the first century as in the twentieth century. No, consciousness changes age to age.[3] Clearly, we are
speaking to a different human consciousness than addressed
by the apostles or by St. Augustine or even by priests and
ministers a mere century ago. Look at paintings from the Age
of Reason they all display the same perspective. They are
painted as if by a third-person objective viewer; in a way, they
are a testimony to the style of the age, rationalism.[4] The world
is viewed as "out there" in careful detail, ordered by detached
objective reason. But wander any art gallery these days, in
New York, London, or Paris, and the canvases are quite different. In a single painting may be several perspectives, angles of
vision superimposed one upon another, acknowledging the
truth of human relativity. Moreover, artists these days have a
much wider definition of reality than artists who were painting the objective "thereness" of rationalism. Artists now are
opening up a world beyond the objective, a world that includes memories and fantasies, swirls of feeling and strange
compelling social myths.[5] Are not memories, myths, fantasies,
feelings, hopes, and the like all components of human reality
at any given moment, even though they do not register on
film or record on tape?

The same sort of change has occurred in fiction, hasn't it?
William Makepeace Thackeray could describe the world of
Becky Sharp in *Vanity Fair* by telling a third-person chronological story from start to finish, viewing everything that happened, "dear reader," as if he were the eyes and ears of God.[6]
But the Victorian novel is no more. Instead, we have seen tem-
poral structures bridged in William Faulkner's *The Sound and
the Fury*, where events seem to be recalled from different
times by the consciousness of different characters—but all
jumbled in the present.[7] Or, we have seen how angles of vision can vary, as when Lawrence Durrell writes four novels,
each from the perspective of a different character, but each fo-
cused on exactly the same events.[8] Nowadays, authors imitate
consciousness—memories merge and fantasies occur; day-
dreams, feelings, urges all happen simultaneously even as we
meet and speak with others in a present-tense world.[9] So,
guess what? We live at a time when definitions of reality are

wider and more complex than in earlier eras. The rationalist, scientific worldview is fading fast; we realize now, as not before, that reality is beyond both objective and subjective categories. Reality is defined by consciousness.[10]

When a world's understanding of reality changes, so does language—or vice versa.[11] Every major language family in the world has been changing radically since the beginning of the present century. Dwight Macdonald has observed that the English language was shrinking until the late 1950s—shrinking and becoming more abstracted. Of approximately 450,000 words in the big *Webster's New International Dictionary* in 1934, more than 150,000 words may have dropped from common vocabulary in the first half of the century. Then, since the 1960s, though another 50,000 words may have slipped away, language began to enlarge again—global words invaded common English, and subcultural speech was heard and repeated—the language began to enlarge again and to become much more metaphorically alive. Some lexographers suppose that more than half the standard vocabulary will have altered in less than a century. Since Wilhelm von Humboldt we have known that worldviews are embodied in language.[12] So what's going on in the world today? Why, a whole wide world is changing its mind! We live in the midst of an epochal event similar in scope to the collapse of the Greco-Roman world and the fragmentation of the medieval synthesis. No wonder we reissue dictionaries and rewrite our liturgies. To repeat: We must find a way to preach in a world that is changing its mind.

Note the word "changing": Our consciousness is changing and is not yet fixed, or even close to taking shape. Rather obviously, we live "between the times" in the midst of tumbling paradigms. Normally, preaching has method as well as inherited rhetorical conventions left over from the high periods of cultural synthesis. For example, early in the 1800s, Bishop Whately framed a way of speaking for an Enlightenment culture that has lasted and, liberally borrowed by nineteenth-century homileticians, is still very much in pulpit practice.[13] Yet, in times of change such as our own age, rhetorical–homiletic patterns form anew. Augustine wrote in a time of radical change and shaped homiletic tradition for the medieval church. The Reformers, Luther and Calvin, also preached in a turbulent era and set precedents for years of Protestant preaching. The task of our age is not only to speak the gospel but also to find and form new ways of preaching for an emerging new human consciousness. Biblical study is now working beyond the supposed objective rationalism of historical-critical method,[14] in structuralism,[15] various literary-critical approaches,[16] rhetorical criticism,[17] reader-response methods after Wolfgang Iser,[18] and even procedures that have been developed from sociologies of knowledge.[19] Likewise, many theologians have moved beyond the neo-orthodoxy of the past fifty years.[20] At minimum, they are Revisionist, if not deliberately post-Protestant. So homiletic method is much more than a how-to program for desperate preachers; it is strategy for the presentation of the gospel in a strange, turbulent new age. Questions of method are not merely practical matters. We are asking how to present the gospel message to an emerging, quite different human consciousness.

Worn-out Preaching Conventions

Many preachers were trained to speak from one-verse texts. Though liturgical tradition provided lections for Catholics, Anglicans, Lutherans, and some others during the 1920s, 1930s, 1940s, and 1950s, single-verse texts were still common—"Esau was an hairy man."[21] If we did not preach from snippets of scripture, we operated with what might be described as a method of distillation. We distilled topics from biblical passages. We looked at some selected biblical passage objectively, and then, as if the passage were a still-life picture, we took out something to preach on, namely, a subject matter, some aspect of the passage as a topic. So, for example, any brief pericope could yield many, many topics. Look at Luke 7:2-10:

> 2Now a certain centurion had a slave who was dear to him, who was sick and about to die. 3Having heard of Jesus, he

sent Elders of the Jews to him, begging him to come and pull his slave through. [4]They came to Jesus earnestly pleading with him, saying, "He is worthy for you to do this, [5]for he loves our country and it was he who built our synagogue for us." [6]And Jesus went with them.

But when he was not far from the house, the centurion sent friends to him, saying, "Lord, don't hassle yourself. I am not worthy for you to come under my roof; [7] . . . but say the word and my boy will be healed. [8]For I too am a man functioning under authority, with soldiers under me. I say to one 'go' and he goes, and to another 'come' and he comes; and to my slave 'do this' and he does it!"

[9]Having heard this, Jesus marveled at him and, turning to the crowd that followed him, said, "I tell you never in Israel have I found such great faith!" [10]And when those who had been sent returned to the house, they found the slave a picture of health.[22]

Preachers could preach on "The Healing Power of Jesus," "The Faith of a Soldier," "Living Under Authority," "We Have Heard of Jesus," "The Secret of a Great Faith," "Just Say the Word," "Love for a Slave," "True Worthiness: God and Country," "On Humility," etc.; the topics from any single pericope can seem endless.[23] Notice how the text offers some sort of controlling biblical authority for preaching—to be exact, not at all!

Methods of distilling topics from passages developed in the eighteenth century with the rise of rationalism.[24] For example, if you dared to preach on the stilling of the storm, some surly rationalist might protest the miracle; but if you distilled a topic from the story—"Our Fears and Jesus" or "God and Nature"—you could cheerfully sidestep the embarrassments of the biblical miracle. What's more, you might even get a reputation for psychological or philosophical acuity at the same time. Not only did the method of distillation avoid embarrassments in the biblical text, but, in itself, it parodied scientific method. After all, scientific method is based on isolation and observation. You isolate an object for study—for example, a pocket watch. You venture a general hypothesis: "Here is a timepiece," and then you follow with "points": [1] "It is round;" [2] "It has numbers;" [3] "It looks cheap," or, whatever. The word "point" is a tip-off, isn't it? In our sermons, we pointed at things; sermons were exercises in rational observation. Most of us were trained in a homiletic method of distillation. If we didn't pick out a single-verse text—"But my brother Esau is an hairy man, but I am a smooth man"—we distilled single topics from chunks of scripture. Remember the usual Lenten sermon series that might feature six or seven brief phrases clipped from something like the parable of the Prodigal Son? What were we doing with scripture? We were chasing down something to preach on.

Well, what did we lose? Why, we lost the whole story. We discarded both narrative structure and, in non-narrative passages, the rhetoric of a structural movement.

Rational homiletics treated biblical passages as if they were still-life pictures. You could study them, comment on the details within the picture, and then take something out of the picture to talk about in a sermon. In our efforts we were supported by erudite historical-critical commentaries. They too isolated a passage and then, verse by verse, explained each detail philologically or historically. Commentaries would often conclude their discussions with a sentence or two on the subject matter they found in the passage.[25] Notice both the "scientific" commentary and the rational preacher regarded the passage as if it were a still-life picture, full of things to isolate and talk about. Oddly enough, the many things to talk about presented themselves, seriatim, as of equal weight. So, in Luke 7:2–11, commentaries might devote more space to a description of the synagogue in Capernaum, or the question of who "elders of the Jews" were, than to a treatment of the centurion's astonishing phrase, "say the word."[26] And we preachers followed along, rather indiscriminately taking something out to feature in our sermons—a title to print in a newspaper notice or the Sunday morning church bulletin.

Truth in Motion

Instead, let us suppose that biblical passages are much more like motion-picture film clips. They are not static, still-life pictures full of things to look at objectively. No, they move like stories, episode by episode; or, they travel along with the give and take of lively conversation, moving from one idea to another; or, they may be designed like poems around an inter-action of images. Suppose that movements, rather than still-life meaning, characterizes any language.[27] We might have to learn to explore scripture in a new way and, yes, to preach quite differently. Meaning occurs in a movement of thought or event; it is never static truth but involves travel from one understanding to another. Older rational homiletics seemed to suppose that preaching dealt in fixed conceptual beliefs. Therefore, sermons helped people align themselves vertically with God's truth—they could "get right with God." But, no, if meaning is structural and structure is shaped by movement of thought or image or event, then we *journey* into truth, going along with God's guiding word.

So instead of point-making sermons, often categorical in de-sign, we will be developing something like scenarios for preach-ing, movements of thought from beginning to end. Often, an older homiletics would distill a topic from a text, let us say "Love," and then develop the subject matter categorically (1) "Love in the family," (2) "Love in the church," (3) "Love in the world," and then sometimes throw in a poem for conclusion!

What's wrong with categorical point-making sermons? Well, they are intrinsically tedious. They are static and didac-tic at the same time. Though a minister can jot down categori-cal points with ease, 1–2–3, people in the pews find such sermons almost impossible to hear. Usually the introduction to a categorical sermon has contained some sort of tip-off, such as a final sentence: "So love is the most important thing we do—in our family life, in our churches, and, yes, out in the world." Such tip-off sentences were considered good form by an older homiletics. Congregations pick up the key sentence and realize that they are in for a three-point categorical sermon; no surprises need be expected. Then, if a first point,

"Love in the family," takes nine minutes, we can expect shuffling nervousness when the preacher—through a series of clumsy "transitional" sentences—shifts to "Love in the church." What, another nine minutes? Sensing restiveness, the preacher will reduce the second point to seven minutes and pad the sermon with more illustrations ("And how to amuse them today?"). Again, when the preacher shifts to a final, "Love in the world," groans from the congregation are almost audible. Then the preacher will cut back to five minutes, three of which will be devoted to an "all-the-stops-pulled-out" emotional illustration that may help to pass the time. Categorical systems are easy, but *only* for clergy. Because they are static and have no moving excitement—What will happen next?—they are hard to listen to in a congregation. The categorical sermon goes back to a rationalist tradition of learning lessons didactically: 1–2–3, a–b–c.

But ask yourself, do you speak of the deepest, dearest moments in your life by listing descriptive categories? No, you tell what happened as a story or you try to open up meaning through a series of interrelated, probing descriptions. We human beings save categorical thinking for trivia, for grocery lists, or sorting laundry—so many bras, so many shirts, so many socks. Do we talk to those we love most intimately in conversational lists?—"Please attend: I love you for the following three good reasons . . ." No, there is sweet give-and-take to loving conversation, a bemused, affectionate banter that speaks and listens and speaks again, moving from subject to subject by picking up clues from one another. What we do not do is to speak categorically. Even schoolrooms have wisely redefined didactic methods for learning. Only the pulpit still clings to "points to be made." But, in preaching the gospel message, we are not speaking some fixed Word of God truth that hangs before us like a poster and that we can discuss by pointing. No, as preachers we are journeying with our people into the mysteries of God, and journeying requires a very different homiletic method.

On Being Form-Critical

We must notice another change. Let us call it the importance of form.[28] Preachers must learn to take form seriously in scripture as well as in sermons. An older homiletics indulged in what might be termed a shell game; meaning was viewed as a kernel hidden within a shell-like form. God's truth could be wrapped up in all kinds of shells. The task of an interpreter was to crack the shell and liberate truth. What were the shells? They were the stories, the parables, the epigrams, the poetry, indeed the words that encased the pithy truth. Form was regarded with a degree of hostility; form was something that hid or at best obscured the truth of God. Fortunately the kernel/shell model has disappeared. Long before Marshall McLuhan, scholars had begun to sense that form is not a disposable shell; no, form *is* part of meaning.[29] For example, would you attempt to write a treatise on thermodynamics as if it were lyric love poetry? No, the results would be astonishing. Likewise, why would you try to preach a parable within a system of categorical points? Most parables have narrative plot. Parables do not contain hidden lessons, some kernel in a storied shell. Thus a newer homiletic will brood over matters of form. Not only will we study the forms of scripture, we will also begin to sense the forms we human beings use every day in our lives.

Actually, most biblical scholars suppose that form is a clue to intention. To say it simply, form is something we choose in order to *do*. Think of the many language forms you bump into every week.[30] "Once upon a time there was a beautiful lady who sat on a bench that, when the sun shone, seemed made of gold . . ."—you are hearing a fairy tale. Or, "Mr. and Mrs. Smith request the pleasure of your company at . . ."—you are reading a formal invitation you must answer. When someone says, "Hey, did ya hear the one about the traveling salesman and the farmer's daughter . . . ," you brace yourself for a raucous joke.[31] Forms are not interchangeable. You can't tell a racy joke as if it were a formal invitation; it simply would not work. Did you pick up the word "work"? The linguistic forms in any culture are designed to *work*; they accomplish

Forms in our everyday Conversations that achieve what Biblical forms wanted to accomplish.

things, they are performative. Perhaps all biblical language is performative; though written down, biblical language is made up of oral forms designed to do. So, can the intentionality of scriptural language be realized within the standard forms of a traditional, point-making sermon? If meaning is not a kernel that can be crammed into any kind of shell, then perhaps we as preachers must find different forms for the very different biblical passages we preach. Think how bracing it might be for pew-sitters if the sermons they hear had different forms— at times sounding like stories, at times moving along from one poetic image to another like verse, or perhaps sounding sometimes like the exchanges in a sharp debate.[32] A modern homiletic will have to attend to matters of appropriate form. Form and meaning are inseparable.

Yet we should not suppose that biblical forms can be imitated in our preaching—a story for a biblical story, a hymnic sermon for a psalm, an imagistic protest poem for some prophetic passage. No, preaching does not dabble in imitative art forms; it is public speaking to a known audience. Preaching must be what it is. Forms of speech that were instrumentally useful in biblical times—forms that were designed to *do*—may not achieve the same ends now. Yes, we must reject the kernel-in-a-shell model that regarded the "shells" as insignificant and therefore interchangeable. But we should not suppose that to preach a passage from Amos, we should construct a poetry of prophetic diatribe. No, we do not imitate forms. Instead, we must seek to discover contemporary forms, forms that in our everyday conversations achieve what the biblical forms wanted to accomplish.

Particular biblical forms may no longer be useful. For example, servants evidently were sent out to different houses to invite guests to a party. To accomplish what the biblical world intended must we hire a fleet of street-running servants? Being biblical does not mean being stupid! These days we send our formal invitations or punch the buttons on a telephone. *Intention* is a clue to forms, not imitation. Yet, while forms may not be similar—a form for a form—it is possible that our language may move along with the same logic as in a biblical form. Thus, when confronted with a biblical narrative, we may decide not to retell a story, but our sermon may move along in response to the biblical material episodically. The structural logic of our sermon may be a narrative logic.

Biblical form may have a deeper purpose. Form shapes hermeneutic response. Form is not only an expression of a speaker's purpose, it may also order a hearer's response. Form tells us how we are to interpret the language we hear and how we may respond. For example, the formal invitation, "Mr. and Mrs. Smith request the pleasure of your company at . . . ," means that we may not chuck the letter in the wastebasket with a dismissive giggle. No, the form of the message indicates we are invited to a special formal occasion and that we are expected to respond formally. Notice that the form tells us *what* we are reading and *how* we should respond. Or, consider the fairy-tale start, "Once upon a time there was a beautiful lady who sat on a bench that, when the sun shone, seemed made of gold. . . . " We hear the words and at once realize we are listening to a fairy tale. Therefore, we suspend historical questions; we do not ask who the lady was or where the bench was located. Likewise, the form involving the traveling salesman and the farmer's daughter tells us that we will be hearing an indelicate joke and should respond appropriately, either by gurgling laughter or by taking offense—dirty jokes can be labored or even abusive. But in every case the form oriented us to the intent of the language and at the same time prepared us to respond in some fashion. Is it possible that sermons may function in much the same way?[33]

Angles of Vision

There is an aspect to form we scarcely notice. We shall call it point of view.[34] We have already mentioned that rationalism viewed reality objectively. Every painting in the Age of Reason seemed to be painted by a detached, dispassionate, third-person observer. Years before, when Giotto painted, canvases were less dimensional but, though flat, featured fluttering angels or crouching demons—artists were not being superstitious; they were painting true reality for a medieval world. In the Age of Reason, the demons and the angels were erased; things were painted as they appeared to be before some keen-eyed objective viewer. Not surprisingly, the compositions of paintings in the seventeenth and early eighteenth centuries are strangely boxed in—"irrational" things were being kept out! Oddly enough, sermons during the period were written from the same objective position. The language of the age was a descriptive language designed to record "thereness." So, at the same time as Protestantism was busy sweeping across the Western world, rationalism was shaping a language designed to exorcise not only the angels and the demons, but also transcendence.

Even today, most sermons speak as if we were observing.[35] For the most part, the language of preaching is still third-person descriptive. So we talk of God as if God were an observable object. We even speak of our own religious experience by describing ourselves objectively. In our speaking, we are much like the early days of motion-picture production. Old films were made with a fixed-point camera in front of which actors moved and spoke their lines. In the past, such filmmaking was admired for its supposed realism. Now we see the old films on late-night television and giggle; they seem quite stagy and artificial. Films now are fashioned by a camera on a moving boom so that angles of vision keep changing; there may be hundreds of such shifts of point of view within a matter of minutes. The reason for shifting camera angles is that human consciousness has changed; we view reality quite differently, from different angles of vision. The relativity of consciousness has already shaped changes in the way we converse with one another. If you wore a tape recorder for a day, you would discover our ordinary conversation displays all kinds of shifts in perspective, as if we were speaking from various angles of vision. We are dealing with a major alteration in human discourse—except in preaching! The usual language of preaching is relentlessly fixed camera, a third-person, objective speech. Perhaps in the future our sermons will travel through a series of moves, each with a different well-defined point of view.[36] After all, for the sake of the gospel, preachers must attempt to speak a language designed to formfit the contemporary shape of human consciousness.

The Myth of "Biblical Preaching"

Before we venture a description of method, we must deal with a kind of shibboleth; let us label it the myth of biblical preaching. The biblical theology movement has dominated our thinking for most of the mid-twentieth century. As a result, many books have been written on "biblical preaching"; specifically on how preachers can move step by step from the Bible passage to a sermon. Many of these works—from Donald Miller to Ernest Best—have been genuinely helpful. They have explained exegetical procedure in great detail—translating, word study, checking related biblical references, doing commentary research, and so forth. They have also described a set of homiletic procedures from initial outlining down to a final speaking of the sermon. But in all such books there seems to be a gap. There's something left out in between. The crucial moment between exegesis and homiletic vision is not described. The shift between the study of a text and the conception of a sermon—perhaps it occurs in a flash of imagination—is never discussed. So alert readers are left with the odd impression that we move from the Bible to a contemporary sermon by some inexplicable magic!

Let us admit the truth: In a way, none of us preach directly from the Bible. Not really. Perhaps the whole notion of biblical preaching is a popular fallacy. Instead, here is what seems to happen. As we translate, study, and consider a text, the structure of the biblical passage forms a contemporary structure of meaning in our consciousness. Most of us are hardly aware of the process occurring. But the words of a text are written in contemporary English and have contemporary experiential word associations. Even if we are fluent in biblical languages, we still translate understandings into our own contemporary language and thought forms. Thus, we may read in the Bible how Jesus talked down a storm on the Sea of Galilee. But, the word "storm" comes into our consciousness along with contemporary word associations—the weather summary on the evening television news with front lines and low-pressure cells and the like, or power outages in our cities, or deciding that we had better move off the porch because of nearby lightning flashes. The crouching fears of a first-century person can never happen in our awareness; we do not cower before divine furies or tremble because demons have stirred the waves. We can think about first-century attitudes, but we cannot have them as our own—original meaning will ever elude us. So we transfer biblical texts into contemporary meaning as we read and study.

Back in the 1960s we engaged in implausible debates over "demythologizing," debates between biblical Barthians and equally biblical Bultmannians.[37] In one way the debates were silly because every preacher automatically demythologizes. We understand through the in-use word associations of our own culture. Thus, contemporary experience comprehends biblical passages. In the immediacy of reading a text, we are already forming a contemporary understanding, our contextual understanding. What do we preach from? We preach from a *contemporary* structure of understanding in consciousness. We have used the term "structure" to indicate that the original material was structural—if a parable, then a narrative structure, if a Pauline passage, then a rhetorical structure. When we translate, study, learn about a passage, a similar structure of *contemporary* understanding is formed. But here is the true state of affairs: We do not preach from the Bible directly. No, instead, every sermon is preached from a contemporary structure of meaning that may have been prompted by studying scripture.

We can preach *about* the Bible. A great many preachers do. Preaching about the Bible has enlarged lately because of the notion of historical revelation; the idea that God is singularly revealed in or through historical events—"the mighty acts of God" was George Ernest Wright's phrase. Probably the "revelation in history" school emerged as a reaction to the nineteenth century. Descriptive sciences were busy demystifying nature, and subsequently Sigmund Freud arrived to dissect the soul; thus, arguments from the natural world or from "varieties of religious experience"[38] were suspect. With a sigh, we turned to historic events that, happily, had been scribbled down in the Bible. Did preachers suppose that homiletic description could restore events to their original revelatory power? Certainly many preachers began sermons with discussion of the Bible, of biblical history, of the biblical *"Sitz im Leben,"* of biblical characters, and so forth. As a result, we now have an odd tension between preaching the Bible's past-tense revelation-through-history and speaking contemporary good news of the Living God!

If we are to preach from scripture, we must banish the then–now splits that disfigure sermons. We wrestle with the Bible in contemporary consciousness and, in so doing, can encounter the God of our lives. Theology has already moved beyond the notion of "mighty acts of God" revelation. Perhaps we preachers must begin to think ourselves out of the revelation-in-history model. Even when we preach from scripture, we are preaching from a structure of meaning—perhaps theological meaning—that has formed in consciousness. We are interpreters. We are hermeneutically active. Preaching can never be a form of biblical recitation if only because the good news is *now!*

Doing a Sermon

Probably the only way to get at method is to take an example. Let us suppose that we must preach an assigned lection, namely, the parable of the Rich Man and Lazarus in Luke 16:19–31.[39] At first glance, the passage seems to be set in structural design—there's a rich man, a poor man, a reversal of positions, a sweaty plea from the rich man, and then a harsh reply from Father Abraham. The shifts in the narrative seem to add up to a five-move sermon. Of course, the parable contains a peculiar addendum, verses 27–31, containing the rich man's request for a warning message to be sent to his five brothers, and Abraham's terse, "If they do not listen to Moses and the prophets, neither will they be convinced even if someone rises from the dead." At the outset, a preacher will have to decide whether to preach the parable itself, ending with verse 26, or to include the addendum. In our discussion, we will limit the parable quite arbitrarily to Luke 16:19–26.[40]

The main task of ministry is meaning~! (handwritten margin note)

You could distill a topic from the text: "Beggars at Our Gates—The Problem of Urban Homelessness"; or, perhaps, "Rich and Poor: A Crisis in Our World Today"; or even, "Charity—Christ's Call to Compassion." The beauty of a distilled topic is that you have no decisions relating to the scope of the text and, in addition, no exegetical homework. But, you will have to live with yourself and with your own carelessness with regard to the scriptures. If we believe that parables are about as close to original "red-letter" words of Christ as we can get, we should bestir ourselves enough to see what the Lord had in mind.[41]

A second problem: Recent parable research has been truly remarkable. Most well-known parables have been reinterpreted, and the reinterpretations appear to be more than plausible. In other words, parables no longer mean what we once thought they meant. We may be dismayed. But why? The main task of ministry is *meaning*. As clergy, we are resident theologians for the people of God, and keeping up with theological disciplines is our job. So, not only will we study the text and consult commentaries, but we also will try to learn of contemporary parable scholarship.[42]

Here is the passage:

[19]Now there was a certain rich man, who used to put on a purple robe with fine linen, and who partied every day, sumptuously. [20]And there was a certain poor man, Lazarus by name, who was dumped down at his gate covered with sores. [21]He longed to be filled with scraps that fell from the rich man's table. But only the dogs came out to lick his sores. [22]It so happened that the poor man died and was carried off by angels to be at ease with Abraham. And the rich man died and was buried. [23]In Hades, suffering torments, he looked up and, in the distance, saw Father Abraham with Lazarus relaxing nearby. [24]Calling out, he said, "Father Abraham, pity me! Send Lazarus to dip the tip of his finger in water and cool my tongue, because I'm suffering in these flames!" [25]But Abraham said, "Child, remember how you received your good things during your lifetime and, likewise, how Lazarus received the bad; now

he is at ease and you are in pain. [26]In any case, there is a great chasm between us and you, firmly fixed, so that anyone wanting to cross from here to you cannot; neither can anyone there cross over to us."

What do we need to know to preach the parable? Structurally, the parable is quite simple. There are two men. One is rich; he dresses in purple and feeds on gourmet foods. The other man is poor; he is too weak to beg, so he lies at the gate to the rich man's house and hopes for scraps of garbage. Wild street dogs lick his sores. Then, the plot turns suddenly. Both men die. The poor man ends up at table with Father Abraham, while the rich man lands in hot Hades. So far the parable's movement is a description first of one man, then of another, followed by a dramatic role reversal.

In Hades, the rich man begs Abraham to send Lazarus with a finger-dip of water to assuage his thirst. But Abraham declares that, No, the request is impossible because "a great chasm has been fixed" between them. Structural options are limited; we have two descriptions, a role reversal in afterlife, and Father Abraham's blunt announcement of a "chasm fixed between." So, in preaching, either you will begin at the beginning and design your sermon to match the episodes in the parable itself, or perhaps you could begin in the afterlife scene and look back at the previous condition of the two characters, before trying to understand Father Abraham's awful pronouncement. Such a scheme would work, but it might reduce the shock of the reversal of roles in the parable. So, at the outset, we will decide to follow the original narrative.[43]

Rereading the Text

Exegetically, there are some nuances we can spot. The rich man has no name! No, he has no identity other than his social station—he has become "richman."[44] He dresses in purple and therefore is probably a *nouveau riche* social climber who aspires to royalty, or possibly a court official.[45] Not only does the rich man party sumptuously, but he does so "every day."

By contrast, the poor man has a name, Lazarus, which ironically means "one whom God helps." Lazarus is a beggar, and at the time of Christ beggars were regarded as sinners. Their poverty was viewed as a form of divine punishment.[46] Lazarus lies outside the rich man's gate and grovels for table scraps in the garbage. He is too weak to ward off vicious wild street dogs who lick his sores and may be waiting to gnaw his bones.[47] The contrast between the rich man in his mansion and the poor man outside the gate is carefully drawn.

But, watch out, keep an eye on the symbol of the gate.

The next section of the parable is denoted by a favorite Lukan storytelling phrase, "It so happened that . . ." Suddenly positions are reversed. The poor man, Lazarus, is borne by angels to "the bosom of Abraham." The phrase suggests intimacy; Lazarus is under the protection of Abraham. But more likely it indicates his place at a banquet table next to host Abraham. Lazarus, who scrounged for scraps of garbage on earth, is now feasting in an afterlife. And, of course, the rich man, who had once partied every day, now cries out for a single drop of water. Please note, the rich man *never* addresses Lazarus directly, even in afterlife. No, he regards Lazarus as slave class and therefore asks Abraham to order Lazarus to provide moisture for his lips.

Some hearers have been struck by the fact that rich and poor are reversed in an imagined afterlife without any moral distinctions being drawn. Is the rich man condemned simply by his being rich? And is the poor man rewarded on the basis of nothing more than his poverty? Answer: Yes, probably. Remember Luke's version of the Beatitudes in Luke 6:20–25:

> Blessed are you who are poor,
>> for yours is the kingdom of God.
> Blessed are you who are hungry now,
>> for you will be filled.

Luke's subsequent words with regard to the rich are unreservedly harsh:

> But woe to you who are rich,
>> for you have received your consolation.

> Woe to you who are full now,
> for you will be hungry.

Luke's attitude toward wealth is stern indeed. Most Protestant preachers speak of money as neutral, something that can be used for good or evil—thus appeasing affluent Christians; but for Luke, quite rightly, cash seems to be an evil per se.[48]

We have mentioned the fence and the gate. Bernard Brandon Scott aptly quotes a line from Robert Frost: "Something there is that doesn't love a wall."[49] The rich man could have walked through the gate and acknowledged Lazarus, his neighbor. He did not, and he does not, even in afterlife. He will not acknowledge the beggar as a neighbor. So, the gate that separated the rich man and Lazarus turns upside down: "There is a great chasm between us and you, firmly fixed," says Father Abraham! The "something that doesn't love a wall" is love, the love that God is and that God enjoins.

Moving toward a Sermon

So how to design a sermon? The sermon will need an Introduction and a Conclusion and in between a series of moves. Probably we will need an Introduction that will define the parable's genre. Possibly something such as the following:

> Have you ever heard a joke about the "pearly gates." There used to be stories about the Irishmen, Pat and Mike, meeting St. Peter at heaven's gate. Well, guess what? There were stories about heavenly hereafter at the time of Christ. Perhaps Jesus borrowed one of them, for he told a story about a rich man and a beggar meeting Abraham in the afterlife. Listen once again to the strange parable of Jesus.

Why would we want such an Introduction? Because we must get rid of any tendency to read any literal references to an afterlife in the parable. The parable proves absolutely nothing about a hereafter; it does not document either heaven or hell. Every congregation harbors a few Christians who are eager to establish hell, particularly for other sinners. No, Jesus is merely playing around with a folktale tradition.[50]

Now, the first two paragraphs of your sermon will introduce the two characters in a kind of storytelling style. A preacher need not stick to a "daily life in Bible times" treatment of the two characters. Obviously, the contrast will be more telling if you move the figures into our twentieth-century world. In America today, there are more than three million homeless people. In the past two decades, the rich have become richer while the poor have multiplied in poverty.[51] At the same time, Americans are very much into conspicuous consumption—fine wines and gourmet foods are available in most urban shopping malls. So description will be easy. Naturally, you will be smart enough to begin and end each of these moves with mention of the gate—"Behind a high gate, a rich man lived . . . ," "Outside the gate, down on the ground, a beggar lay. . . ." Adjectives you apply to the fence gate can show up later attached to the chasm! You don't need to labor the message when you can make it happen!

There is an old Romanesque stone carving of the parable. In an upper right hand corner is the rich man in his flowing robes at table, a goblet held high in celebration. Down in a left hand corner, helplessly lying on his back, is the beggar, Lazarus. Wild dogs are lined up, waiting. But the carver had read the parable well, for diagonally there is a wide sweep of stone like a wall dividing the two figures.[52]

Your third move can be surprised by the reversal. Does God automatically reward the poor of the world? In capitalist countries, we still tend to regard poverty as the ultimate sin; to us, people on welfare are freeloaders at best. But Lazarus ends up feasting with Father Abraham as if he were a good and faithful Jew—which, by the way, the parable does *not* say. And the rich man, think of it, does he end up in hell simply because he's rich?

A fourth move will introduce the pleading by the rich man. Now he appears to be down, but looking up to Lazarus. Maybe we rich nations can never understand the agony of the poor until somehow we suffer hunger and thirst. Then suddenly we cry out for compassion. The problem for most congregations is

Preaching and Method

that they view world poverty on the television screen; they see it from the comfort of their all-American homes. Poverty is elsewhere—Somalia or Ethiopia—poverty is always distant. Of course, "in the distance" describes the perspective of the rich man in Hades!

Finally we will face Abraham's terrible reply. We build fences to protect ourselves from hearing the cry of the hungry, from catching sight of desperate people like Lazarus around us. Tragically, fences can become eschatologically permanent. Most preachers seek to avoid preaching about ultimate penalties. After all, we are justified by grace and thus are we not assured of God's permanent affection? If we have God's permanent affection—the sunny smile on the "God Loves You" button—then the whole notion of ultimate penalty is erased forever; God accepts us as is! But we forget; though we are justified by grace, we are still judged by works and, according to Matt. 25:31–46, works involve feeding our neighbors who are hungry, clothing those who are ragged, and providing home in our homes for the homeless who live hidden on the other side of fences we have built. Remember how in a recent West Coast quake a thruway that had divided a rich neighborhood from a poor one collapsed, turning into an impenetrable barrier. So, in the parable, what was once a wall with a gate to pass through becomes a chasm driven down unimaginable depths. Human carelessness can harden.

So what can we do? The original parable ends hopelessly with a fixed chasm dividing the rich man and Lazarus. But the parable is surely told to stir concern for the poor who, whether we wish to acknowledge them or not, are our kinfolk. How would we rewrite the parable if we could? Would we not walk out of ourselves into a world where people hunger and thirst and claim them in love as our brothers and sisters—which, of course, in God's sight they are. Perhaps then the walls could come tumbling down.

Think of it, the gate of our everyday indifference is a gate to and from heaven!

The Gate of our everyday existence
existence is the gate to + from
heaven.

Hermeneutic Strategies

At the outset, a hermeneutic observation: You will not merely retell the story as a storyteller, even in a contemporary way. You are *not* a storyteller, you are a preacher speaking to people you know and who know you. So you will not speak an updated parable without comment as if a story would do the trick all by itself. But neither will you look at the parable and talk about it as an object of study. A third-person objective discussion of parables will prevent them from getting to us. No, the solution for most parables is to preach as though we and our congregation were hearing and reacting to the movement of the parable together. Such a hermeneutic posture will permit the parable to unfold in consciousness, episode by episode, doing what it is designed to do. At the same time, the strategy of hearing and reacting together will allow us to talk to our congregation and to represent congregational attitudes in a fairly natural fashion.[53] So, to borrow another phrase from Fred Craddock, let us try "overhearing the gospel" together.[54]

Also, observe: No didactic points are made.[55] Instead, you let the structural movement of the parable do its intended work. Oh yes, you help it along. For you define each episode sharply like separate scenes in a drama—you never smooth transitions like a storyteller. Parables, as Bertolt Brecht surmised,[56] are closer to sharply defined scenes in a drama than to the smoothed-out flow of storytelling. And, in your sermon, you will deliberately picture the rich man and Lazarus, locating them in imaginative space; they are defined by up and down and in and out. Of course, you will carefully design the gate symbol, letting the fenced gate enlarge in your sermon, for it is central to the parable's meaning. But you will let the structure happen, scene by scene, so that profound meaning will result. You will not need to hand out a pedantic moral to the story—"now, dear children, what do we learn from this edifying story?" No, *with* your congregation, you will struggle to grasp the parable and to understand how it may be trying to shape our lives. Parables do *not* have lessons. Instead, you will be letting the parable *do* what it may want to do.

sharp

98

Can you sense that preparing sermons can be enthralling, yes, and even fun? Think of approaching texts not aiming to "take out something to preach on," or even asking what teaching, what kernel of God's truth is to be found within the shell of the passage. No, the question you will ask is much more likely to be, "What's going on here?" Or, perhaps, "What does the language want my sermon to do?" Then, maybe, sermons will be exciting again, not only for you who preach, but for your patient neighbors in the pews.

What have we argued? We've asked for structural movement—no static point-making sermons, please. And we've urged you to think of preaching not only as instruction but also as doing what the scriptures want done! A faithful priest or minister will try to let scripture fulfill itself through preaching. And, of course, you will choose vivid imagery because nowadays people think through imaging. Homiletic method has to change because, surprisingly enough, we have.

use vivid imagery

How is this story trying to shape our live?

What's going on here? What does the language want my sermon to do?

Afterword: Looking toward a Future

Some months ago a fortune-teller was interviewed on television: "How can you know the future?" she was asked. The fortune-teller told how she predicted people's future. "You look people over," she said. "You study the palms of their hands. You listen to them talk about themselves." Then, she said: "You get signals from the future!" Well, here we are on the verge of a twenty-first century. Is there any way for us to peer into the future, the future of preaching? The fortune-teller was right. All we can do is to look at our land. Yes, and listen to the way people talk. Then perhaps we too will get signals from the future. What will preaching be in the twenty-first century? What can we expect from the pulpit?

A Different World

We have argued that the cultural trauma we are now going through is not merely another generational change, the 1900s to the 2000s. Most century changes are about as radical as turning the page on a calendar; nothing seems to be much different. But we are now undergoing one of those moments in human history when major paradigm shifts occur. Our age is experiencing events similar to those at the collapse of the Greco-Roman culture or the dissolution of the medieval synthesis. As Bob Dylan sang in the 1960s, "The times they are a-changin'."[1] We live in a transitional time when, apparently, the whole wide world is busy changing its mind.

Some of the changes will be political. Look around: So-called third- and fourth-world peoples are stretching awake and showing eager initiative while, at the same time, Western power appears to be crumbling. Civilizations do rise and fall; today's skyscrapers will be tomorrow's dust. Is anyone naive enough to suppose that American power, particularly American economic power, can possibly last forever?[2] In the future, multinational corporations may threaten human freedoms because few nations will have the clout to control their enlarging power.[3] But then, happily, nationalism itself should be on the wane. After all, from the viewpoint of the gospel, patriotism was always a bad idea. So we can expect a troubled world, full of sudden change and surly terrors, to continue. Cultural upheavals on a worldwide scale do not happen overnight. World change involves rewriting the atlas, yes, but also reconceiving political systems, social patterns—family, work, justice, power—and ecclesial life as well. Just as feudal enclaves gave way to national states, so we can expect quite different political structures in the future that may or may not imitate all-American forms of democracy. Likewise, medieval cathedrals gave way to a scatter of "Church Street" churches all over the world; presumably, the patterns of a new religious life are not yet in view.

Will preaching continue in centuries to come? Yes, obviously, preaching will continue in some form as long as the evangelical work of the church is part of God's great design for the world's redemption. But *how* preaching will continue is difficult to predict. Obviously, a white-European preaching tradition may be a thing of the past. Think of it, we will no longer hear Presbyterians roll their r's and wax nostalgic over the greeeeeaaaat Scottish pulpit tradition. Of course, we will no longer hear Methodists touting John Wesley, Lutherans applauding Luther's eloquence, or Baptists cheering the pulpit intensities of Dr. Billy Graham. The one unassailable fact

about the future is that it will not be white and it will not be
Anglo! No, many sociologists are predicting that by the year
2030 America will be predominantly African American and
Spanish-speaking.[4] White Protestant people will be a distinct
minority. Because most mainline churches have only a small
percentage of members who are African American or His-
panic, the future of such religious bodies is uncertain. Yes, the
gospel will be preached, but patterns of preaching, the
homiletics of the future, will form somewhere, somehow beyond current proponents. American Christianity will startle
Harold Bloom, whose *The American Religion* seemed to conceive a future taken over by the bustling energy of Mormons
and Southern Baptists.[5] No, the population statistics seem to
say American religious life will be determined by the social
emergence of African-American churches and the cultural
spread of a Spanish-speaking religious life.[6] Even mainline
churches will be changed as population patterns alter.[7] Nevertheless, because the gospel is truth of God, it will be spoken.

We must face another change. America is rapidly becoming
a global society.[8] We buy Chinese foods in our supermarkets
and French wines from our liquor stores. Soon we will be able
to shop for different religions. A number of religious buildings
are built annually in Nashville, a city sometimes labeled "The
Buckle on the Bible Belt." Nashville is a city of steeples. But
many of the new buildings last year were dedicated to non-
Christian religions. So Nashville now has Buddist temples, Islamic mosques, and even a building for Eckankar. On a major
artery, motorists can read a sign advising them to say "HU"
and "open our hearts." Remember that Nashville is scarcely a
northern urban-mix sort of city; it is nestled in the Tennessee
hills below the Mason-Dixon line. Religious pluralism is defining our communities. Isn't Dearborn, Michigan, now more
than 30 percent Muslim? But American clergy, Catholic and
Protestant alike, are scarcely equipped to cope with religious
diversity. Many Protestants have been taught by Barth to distinguish Christianity, a biblical *faith,* from the "religions."[9] But
down "Church Street" America are new neighbors now,
whose spirituality is often awesome, carrying copies of the
Koran or singing mantras. Some Christians are nonplussed,

but wisely others are beginning to do their homework so they can be understanding neighbors.[10] Suffice it to say, the context in which we preach is changing, and changing rapidly.

A Backward Look

Could anyone back in 1894 have envisioned preaching in the twentieth century? Probably not. At the end of the nineteenth century divisions existed that are still with us. American village churches that had pushed west from New England or Pennsylvania were concerned with public morality, while social gospelers called for liberation from ungoverned economic oppression, and evangelists spoke to convert huge crowds in Southern fields or city temples. The split between liberals and conservatives seemed to emerge after the Civil War and to define preaching into the start of the twentieth century.[11] But could anyone in the nineteenth century have imagined Karl Barth or Harry Emerson Fosdick or Martin Luther King Jr.? While many preaching patterns were inherited from the nineteenth century, nevertheless Barth, Fosdick, and King have defined the American pulpit in our own age. Fosdick turned to what was called the "new psychology"; Barth returned to a Word of God Bible; and King, surely God's prophetic voice, changed the nation. Three figures patterned our preaching in mid-twentieth century.[12]

Harry Emerson Fosdick turned away from what he considered usual expository preaching; it was, he argued, not only tedious but irrelevant. "Only the preacher," he wrote, "proceeds . . . on the idea that folk come to church desperately anxious to discover what happened to the Jebusites."[13] Despite his social-gospel credentials, Fosdick seemed gradually to turn away from public affairs, from preaching that talked about "American foreign policy, the new aviation, or the latest book."[14] So what did he pursue? "A sermon is meant to meet . . . needs," wrote Fosdick, "the sins and shames, the doubts and anxieties that fill the pews." Even when a preacher speaks to thousands, he observed, the preacher "speaks to them as individuals and is still a personal counselor."[15] Harry Emerson

Fosdick turned to psychological problems, and in his wake we have therapeutic pulpits across the nation. Psychological analysis seems to have replaced theology in many, many churches. Like Fosdick, therapeutic preachers are genuinely concerned to be both relevant and helpful. They know that people these days struggle with inward problems—with doubts and fears and hurts and hates and guilts. But if the pulpit preaches a God no larger than the reflection of contemporary psychological problems, the pulpit will not preach the great God disclosed in Jesus Christ. Though justified by caring, the therapeutic pulpit may have betrayed its prophetic calling.

Karl Barth was a different influence. Appalled by sold-out Christianity in Germany under the Kaiser, he turned back to the Bible. What else, he argued, could preserve God's truth from being co-opted by every passing cultural fad. Preachers, Barth wrote, must "accept the necessity of expounding the Book and nothing else."[16] Barth rejected any real conversation with the culture or concern for relevancies of human event. The old shibboleth to the effect that Barth advised preachers to read the Bible with one eye and the newspaper with the other is not quite true; on Sunday mornings, Barth seemed to fold up his newspaper and toss it aside. According to Barth, scripture is Word of God and thus the only reliable basis for preaching, all preaching. The content of sermons should be biblical—so much so that any concern over contemporary relevance was suspect. By Barth's logic, Bishop Desmond Tutu of South Africa should be reprimanded for biblical unfaithfulness because in his sermons he spoke out against apartheid! But Barth's influence on American preaching has been great. We have become compulsively biblical preachers. But in the process have we lost touch with ongoing human life?

What about Martin Luther King Jr.? He wrote little about preaching; what he did was preach. But in Martin Luther King Jr., a somewhat isolated black church entered into the forum of American society and, armed by the Spirit of God, told the truth. King represents a prophetic voice, a liberation voice that is neither Barth nor Fosdick, neither a compulsive biblicism nor a personal therapeutic,[17] but a voice much more in tune with the rising expectations of third- and fourth-world peoples, a voice that announced the future of God and then added the prophetic word "Now!" A vision of the kingdom of God gave energy to Martin Luther King Jr.'s preaching. What made King more than a mere "social gospeler" was the breadth of his vision as well as the certainty of his being called by the Lord.[18] White church people listened—after all, he was speaking their religious language—and some responded, but many separated themselves from his vision by labeling him "black." So even today, King is probably admired more in rising third-world places than in our still-racist America.

So much for a rehearsal of the past, a brief look at twentieth-century preaching, Barth, Fosdick, and King—biblicism, therapy, and visions of liberation. But, of the three, King is the preacher whose words may still echo in pulpits of the next century.

"The Times They Are a-Changin'"

Now let's turn around and peer cautiously into the future. Are you ready to read the fortune of the twenty-first century? Some things seem clear on the basis of trends now forming. Let us line them out.

Surely, we are moving into a new *evangelical* age; the word is "evangelical" not "evangelicalist." Once more we will have to turn and converse with the secular world. Once more we will have to preach the gospel beyond church walls. Sermons will be both more evangelical and, above all, more apologetic. For nearly fifty years there has been some tendency to regard the secular world "out there" as the enemy of biblical faith. In the thought of Karl Barth, the Bible alone was the source of revelation; there was no other knowledge of God, no natural theology, no insights, no wisdoms, no truth to be gleaned from the human world. In a way, the world was regarded as an adversary. Therefore, preachers were *not* called to relate to the world, but simply to expound biblical truth to the faithful in church. The end of the line seems to be a recent "Kudzu" comic strip in which the Rev. Will B. Dunn's church basketball team, the Holy Rollers, was pitted against an opposing team called the Secular Humanists.[19] If nothing else, the adversary position lacks courtesy. Once more we must learn to converse with the mind of our age and we must do so with genuine love and respect; remember John 3:16 is still in the Bible—"God so loved the world." We must once more learn to listen and speak, to speak and listen to the world God loves. Instead of busing people into our churches where the Bibles are, we are going to have to get ourselves out into the social world with nothing more than good sense and the gospel message. In the next century, we will be moving into an era of evangelism.

Of course, we are bound to converse with other religious groups as well. In a world culture, which is surely happening, Islamic religion will not be an alien unknown on the other side of the world; instead, Islam may move next door on Church Street in our American villages. We can no longer assume that other religions are the enemy because they don't clutch the same Bible as we do. Long, long ago, the Cappadocian Christian leaders affirmed the breadth of the Holy Spirit working out God's purposes in all things.[20] Surely the Spirit is active in our world, not only in Christian enclaves, but in political parties, liberation movements, and, yes, of course, other religions. So we will seek the Spirit, the same Spirit that was with Christ Jesus, as we converse with our religious friends, learning from them. Christian apologetics explaining ourselves in the language of the secular age, is part of evangelism. But good evangelism cannot happen if we assume enmity. Family affection within the human family is the only appropriate context of evangelism.

To be truly evangelical, we must counter the impulse toward self-preservation that seems to live in our churches these days. Most white mainline Protestant churches are desperately into survival. We are perfectly willing to see ourselves as resident aliens in a hostile secular world who above all must shore up identity. But Jesus Christ is, I think, explicit: "For those who want to save their life will lose it, and those who lose their life for my sake, and for the sake of the gospel, will save it." I assume the words of Christ address churches and denominations as well as Christian persons. Evangelism is always risky; you can—no, inevitably you *will*—lose yourself.

The gospel message will be redefined in cultural encounters. So we are called to preach the gospel in the world and leave the preservation of the church to God's good graces. After all, the commissions in the Bible do *not* say, "Go out into the world and hold onto yourselves!"

Because evangelism is primarily a lay activity, we must train our people. We are not referring to church-growth gimmickry, program hype, or pamphleteering. Nor are we endorsing dreadful training sessions on "how to bring Jesus to friends and neighbors." No, if our age accepts a number of tacit assumptions with regard to human nature, human purpose, the uses of power, and goodness knows what else, we will have to examine the assumptions of secularity, a secularity in which we ourselves live and work. And, we will have to think through ways in which we can begin to get a faith-foot into the secular door. We will begin to train our people for an apologetic task. After all, in our age people who believe in the Christian myth are bound to be regarded as somewhat peculiar. So, once more, we will explain ourselves, not by quoting Bible verses to a world that may not accept the Bible as anything special, but by using the common secular language in which we live and by invoking God within structures of contemporary intelligence. Most denominational programs of evangelism are an embarrassment at best or, at worst, a self-interested institutional sales spiel. Christians can be sweet brazen people, but they need not be dumb. We will have to inaugurate what might be termed a lay homiletic.

Perhaps we must add a word of caution. The church is primarily a witness in the world; we tell good news of God. But we cannot ignore the contexts in which our speaking occurs. If we preach to persons who are victims of grinding poverty with no concern for social solutions to their poverty, as if saving souls had nothing to do with food on the table, we will misrepresent Jesus Christ. Did not Marx castigate the church for handing out pie-in-the-sky social salvation to the poor and thus binding them in their poverty?[21] No, evangelism can be done only in solidarity with the victims of earth and is bound to involve taking on the powers that be.[22] The split in many North American congregations between activists and pietists seems to prevent authentic evangelism, for true evangelism goes hand in hand with social concern. Christianity is now multiplying in Africa, Asia, and in the barrios of South America, but is doing so within the context of an active liberation theology. American Christianity is lush. There can be no real evangelism without yielding both the money and the power that American Christianity represents. Remember, Christ cannot be truly preached except in "solidarity with victims."[23]

Welcome to a Wider World

Another caveat: In the future, we will make a move from psychological personalism to social consciousness. We are beginning to sense that we wrestle with principalities and powers and not merely phobias, depressions, and anxiety neuroses. Did you notice that the Academy of Parish Clergy voted Walter Wink's third volume on the "Powers that Be" the most important book for ministers during 1992?[24] The academy was quite right, for after a half century dominated by the rise of a psychological paradigm, we are starting to realize that the gospel is bigger than something called personal salvation. Clearly the Christian scriptures see Christ as a cosmic savior; he doesn't merely save individual souls, a gnostic heresy at best: he saves the entire human enterprise, indeed, the universe. We're beginning to see that the gospel must address a wider social world. Yes, the gospel speaks to me in my self-awareness as a sinner. But as detective story author Ross Mac-Donald, an obvious Calvinist, once observed, "The current of guilt flow[s] in a closed circuit . . . "; it happens *among* our common lives and is never individual.[25] Yes, the gospel may well call me personally to believe and repent. But surely the gospel may also call General Motors to repentance or, yes, the Pentagon and the United States of America. People now feel trapped in systems that are both huge and sinful. We have begun to realize that sin is a captivity; we sinners live in bondage.

Thus when Christians announce salvation, they are not merely touting a payoff hereafter, or some right-now, deeply felt, inner well-being. No, they are speaking of liberation. The promise of Christian salvation is the hope of being set free not simply from inner compulsions—error, depression, binding fantasies, and foolishness—which are problems enough, but of liberation from the systems, social attitudes, customs, and oppressions that hold us captive. Insurance-policy preaching, urging people to come find Jesus and ensure an eternal future, isn't Christian at all; it is merely an appeal to narrow self-interest. On television, there are congregations told that as believers they are ticketed for a heavenly resort, while their unbelieving friends, well, too bad about them. The god such preaching represents is not the God of biblical faith, but a god whose name is SCAM.[26] But, inner-peace preachers, Luther labeled them dream preachers, may also be deceptive. Yes, faith in the God of Jesus Christ is surely a source of inner reconciliation; in God we can live arm in arm with our own souls. But, such peace can be solipsistic if it does not include realism with regard to continuing stress—the context of our lives is ever troubling—and if it does not lead to social liberation. Calvin is quite right; salvation is a promise. Our salvation is social and ultimately eschatological.

So once more we will turn to a preaching of the kingdom of God. Now, talk of the kingdom of God to twentieth-century neo-orthodoxy is a form of heresy; the kingdom of God is regarded as a turn-of-the-century liberal invention, and the word liberal these days is frequently said with a sneer. But Jesus' preaching was filled with news of the kingdom, and we who preach are called to share his message. How many parables of Jesus begin, "The kingdom of God is like . . . "? And are not the Beatitudes a charter of God's promised rule? Through the centuries, like a pendulum swing, the preaching of the church has shifted back and forth between preaching Jesus and preaching good news of the Kingdom, God's new social order. First-century evangelism was probably an invitation to come join the new humanity, a new creation begun in the second Adam, Jesus Christ? Certainly evangelism in the early church was not a plea to have some sort of personal relationship with Jesus, whatever such a phrase may mean. Now at the weary end of the Protestant Era, as an epoch that began with the Reformation is ending, we are called to preach social vision. Prediction: In the twenty-first century we will recover the gospel of the kingdom, God's new order. In the future, preaching will be eschatological rather than existential, and social rather than solipsistic.

A Turn to Theology

Here is a difficult prediction: We will turn back once more to theology. While theology will scarcely triumph on American university campuses or wend its way dramatically into the American cultural mind, once more it will become crucial in the lives of preachers. Theology and homiletics will come together again. Earlier, we discussed the rise of the biblical theology movement, which in many ways was quite hostile to systematic theology. The movement regarded theology as Greek rather than honest, existential Hebrew-biblical thought; and the God of the theologians was *to on*, an ontological abstraction, not the personal God of the Bible. Did we need theology? No. After all, we had our Bibles and could distill biblical understandings without recourse to speculative thinking. Such an attitude was rapidly endorsed by the preaching clergy. After all, the Bible in and of itself was enough of a theological library for any pulpiteer. Oh, there was a huge supporting literature; "The Bible's Understanding of . . . " books flourished. But handing out "The Bible's Understanding of . . . " to agonized human beings who cry out for meaning in an often meaningless contemporary world was simply not adequate. The *primary* task of ministry is not caring, for all kinds of people can offer devoted care; nor is it counseling, for there are able professionals who counsel; nor is it church management, for managers abound. No, the primary task of ministry is *meaning*. If we are ministers of meaning, then we had better learn to think theologically.

Can we Protestants begin to admit that the Bible is, in and of itself, insufficient? The Bible is surely a gift of God, but it is not a magic book. The Bible must be interpreted. All we have to do is to recall the Bible in action with Branch Davidians in Waco,

Texas, in 1993, or the Bible as an object of contention in the ongoing authority fights of the Southern Baptist Convention to realize that the crucial question is not "What does the Bible say?," but "How and by whom is the Bible interpreted?" As Luther observed centuries ago, "Even the devil can quote scripture!" Certainly in the late twentieth-century American church, trapped between a fundamentalist right wing and a charismatic left wing, the issue of who reads the Bible is obvious. Long ago, Rudolf Bultmann raised the question of "pre-understanding," arguing quite rightly that the Bible is read within structures of understanding that are brought to the text.[27] No wonder that Reformers, Luther and Calvin, were prolific theologians; they were attempting to provide pre-understanding for the interpretation of scripture. But of late we have adulated scripture, seemingly certain the words will be both clear and compelling. "The Bible says . . . ," we have chanted, oblivious to the obvious fact that our social location, our religious convictions, our cultural prejudices, all interpret the Bible. Paul Ricoeur speaks of a "hermeneutics of suspicion," and we must listen.[28] Theology reads scripture but, in an age that has neglected theology, social ideologies will read scripture instead.

But theology is not merely a supplied pre-understanding that reads the Bible. We live at a time when events crowd our headlines and the flicker of CNN News continuously records human happenings minute by minute, day by day. We are assailed by goings on. If we must have a hermeneutic of scripture, shall we not also need a hermeneutic of human situations?[29] The television screen deceives us. We begin to suppose that we can live looking on life as detached observers.[30] But our knowledge of God is both expressed and formed in action—the vogue word these days is "praxis." Preaching does not merely interpret biblical texts; preaching is a ministry of meaning, and meaning in the midst of our confusing world is surely a pulpit vocation; we must help congregations to discern the times. Theology articulates faith in contemporary language and in relation to contemporary structures of thought. If preaching is to interpret what is going on, then it must think theologically over events and issues. Biblical preaching has been remarkably isolated. As a result, the average parish program has a gaggle of Bible study groups for human beings who have little experience thinking theologically. For the future, every church will have to install courses in Remedial Theology!

On Learning to Preach All Over Again

We provided an earlier chapter on method. In the chapter, we rehearsed the preaching of a biblical passage, the rich man and Lazarus. But are we moving toward a time when much of the church's speaking will not commence from biblical passages, not even in liturgical settings. The overall Christian community in America appears to be shrinking. In such moments, we are tempted to withdraw into our Bible-study circles and preserve our souls. But as we shrink, we can either become a somewhat self-righteous cultural anachronism, or we can reach out with the gospel message. The need to speak to the world and thus to human situations in the world may move us toward a different homiletics. Our preaching may well become much more oral and immediate. But if we are wise, it will not become less rhetorical. Rhetoric is a speaker's wisdom that is based on how the language works and, more urgently, how human beings understand. For the future, the field of homiletics will have to return and be renewed by conversations with contemporary rhetoricians. People are thinking, understanding, and speaking in ways that belie the homiletic textbooks we have inherited from the past. So we need to think out the rhetorical ways and means appropriate to contemporary consciousness, a task that ought to keep both homileticians and practicing preachers busy.

In learning how to preach the gospel in a new way, those of us who represent a white Protestant culture must be willing to learn from African-American preaching and from the declarative traditions of the Spanish-speaking community. The voices of Christians worldwide will be our schoolroom. Christians in other lands are often wise in wonderful ways when it comes to the presentation of the gospel, particularly in alien cultural contexts.[31] We must learn to listen to the Asian preacher articulating the gospel in relation to "Han." We must study the Christian who speaks to a Buddhist culture in Sri Lanka. Above all, we must attend the speaking of streetwise minority preachers in our own culture. What is our homiletic task in the twentieth century? Perhaps it is learning to preach all over again.

The twenty-first century is almost here. We are preachers of the gospel, a bigger term than preachers of the Bible. People in the twenty-first century will need to hear the gospel message. So, what do we do? Well, we reach out, past our own defensiveness, to see where God may lead us. And surely we delight in seeking new ways to speak, not fixed on the past, but on the unfolding future of God. In every age, the gospel is good news:

> "Now when these things begin to take place, stand up and raise your heads, because your redemption is drawing near. . . . Heaven and earth will pass away, but my words will not pass away." (Luke 21:28, 33)

The words of God are words of liberation.

Abbreviations

CO	*Ioannis Calvani opera quae supersunt omnia.* Ed. Wilhelm Baum, Eduard Cunitz, and Eduard Reuss. 59 vols.)
CR	*Corpus Reformatorum,* vols. 29–87 of CO. C. A. Schwetschke & Son (M. Brühn), 1863–1900.
Institutes	*Calvin: Institutes of Christian Religion.* Ed. John T. McNeill; trans. Ford Lewis Battles. The Library of Christian Classics. Philadelphia: Westminster Press, 1960.
LW	*Luther's Works.* American edition. Ed. Jaroslav Pelikan and Helmut T. Lehmann. 55 vols. St. Louis: Concordia Publishing House; Philadelphia: Fortress Press, 1955–.
ST	Thomas Aquinas, *Summa Theologica.* Trans. Fathers of the English Dominican Province. 3 vols. New York: Benzinger Brothers, 1947–48.
WA	Luther, *Werke.* Kritische Gesamtausgabe. Weimar: H. Bohlau, 1883ff.
WB	*Luther's Primary Works.* Ed. Wace and Buchheim. London, 1896.

Notes

Chapter 1. Preaching and Bible

1. Brevard S. Childs, *Biblical Theology in Crisis* (Philadelphia: Westminster Press, 1970), 32–50, summarizes the biblical theology consensus as a system of beliefs in (1) a theology of the Bible; (2) the intrinsic unity of the Bible's message; (3) the revelation of God in history; (4) a distinctive biblical mentality; and (5) the unique character of the Bible in contrast to its environment.

2. David A. Rausch, "Fundamentalist Origins," *Fundamentalism Today*, ed. Marla J. Selvidge (Elgin, Ill.: Brethren Press, 1984), 11–20.

3. *The International Critical Commentary*, ed. Alfred Plummer, Samuel R. Driver, and Charles Briggs (Edinburgh: T. & T. Clark); *The Interpreter's Bible*, ed. George A. Buttrick (Nashville: Abingdon); *The Anchor Bible*, ed. William F. Albright and David N. Freedman (Garden City, N.Y.: Doubleday & Co.); *The New International Commentary*, ed. J. A. Emerton and C.E.B. Cranfield (Edinburgh: T. & T. Clark); *Interpretation*, ed. James L. Mays (Louisville, Ky.: Westminster/John Knox Press); *Hermeneia: A Critical and Historical Commentary on the Bible*, ed. Frank M. Cross and Helmut Koester (Minneapolis: Fortress Press).

4. According to Brevard Childs (*Biblical Theology in Crisis*, 87), the biblical theology movement is dead: "The Biblical Theology Movement underwent a period of slow dissolution beginning in

the late fifties. The breakdown resulted from pressure inside and outside the movement that brought it to a virtual end as a major force in American theology in the early sixties." Many homileticians have not yet read the obituary.

5. P. T. Forsyth has been labeled a "Barth before Barth" by some interpreters, but I think he represented a somewhat different position; see my review essay, "P. T. Forsyth: The Man, The Preacher's Theologian, Prophet for the Twentieth Century," *Princeton Seminary Bulletin*, n.s. 6 (1985): 231–34. Forsyth's *Positive Preaching and the Modern Mind* has been reprinted along with introductory essays by Donald G. Miller, Browne Barr, and Robert S. Paul: *P. T. Forsyth: The Man, the Preacher's Theologian, Prophet for the Twentieth Century* (Pittsburgh: Pickwick Press, 1981).

6. Karl Barth, *The Word of God and the Word of Man*, trans. Douglas Horton (New York: Harper & Brothers, 1956), 109.

7. Ibid., 116. Note that in the early Barth, human longing and divine response seemed to correlate. Later, Barth denied such correlations and gave less weight to human desire.

8. See Karl Barth, *Church Dogmatics* I/2, trans. G. T. Thomson and Harold Knight (Edinburgh: T. & T. Clark, 1956), chap. 3 and p. 537.

9. Donald G. Miller, *Fire in Thy Mouth* (Nashville: Abingdon Press, 1954), and *The Way to Biblical Preaching* (Nashville: Abingdon Press, 1957).

10. Dietrich Ritschl, *A Theology of Proclamation* (Richmond: John Knox Press, 1960); J.-J. von Allmen, *Preaching and Congregation* (Richmond: John Knox Press, 1962).

11. Reginald Fuller, *The Use of the Bible in Preaching* (Philadelphia: Fortress Press, 1981); Leander Keck, *The Bible in the Pulpit: The Renewal of Biblical Preaching* (Nashville: Abingdon Press, 1978); Ernest Best, *From Text to Sermon: Responsible Use of the New Testament in Preaching* (Atlanta: John Knox Press, 1978); D. Moody Smith, *Interpreting the Gospels for Preaching* (Philadelphia: Fortress Press, 1980).

12. James F. White, *Christian Worship in Transition* (Nashville: Abingdon Press, 1976), chronicles liturgical change in the twentieth century, as does Annibale Bugnini, *The Reform of the Liturgy 1948–1975* (Collegeville, Minn.: Liturgical Press, 1990) from a Catholic point of view. The so-called "Gothic revival" stirred liturgical interest in the 1920s and 1930s, building thousands of stained-glass, pseudo-Gothic churches in American clapboard villages. Then, from the mid-1950s to the early 1970s, denominations

produced a second wave of prayer books, recovering traditions from the Reformation era. Denominations are revising worship materials now with a more conservative and catholic concern. In the 1970s, the Presbyterian *Worshipbook* drew on Vatican II lectionary revision which, in turn, was picked up in publications of the United Church of Christ and the United Methodist Church. More recently, *The Revised Common Lectionary*, prepared by the Consultation on Common Texts, Washington, D.C., and published by Abingdon Press, 1992, presented a further revised list of lectionary readings suitable for ecumenical use. RSV lectionary texts were edited "for experimental and voluntary use" in *An Inclusive-Language Lectionary*, produced by the Division of Education and Ministry of the National Council of the Churches of Christ in the U.S.A., in three volumes (with vols. 1 and 2 revised), 1983–1987.

13. Karl Barth, *Church Dogmatics*, trans. G. W. Bromiley, et. al. (Edinburgh: T. & T. Clark, 1936–75).

14. Karl Barth, *Protestant Thought: From Rousseau to Ritschl* (New York: Harper & Brothers, 1959), 306–54.

15. The phrase is associated with the thought of G. Ernest Wright; see *God Who Acts* (Chicago: Henry Regnery Co., 1952).

16. The connection between preaching and theological purpose is clear in Barth's first attempt at dogmatics, recently published as *The Göttingen Dogmatics: Instruction in the Christian Religion*, vol. 1, ed. H. Reifflen, trans. G. W. Bromiley (Grand Rapids: Eerdmans, 1991), 14–68.

17. Karl Barth, *Homiletics*, trans. Geoffrey W. Bromiley and Donald E. Daniels (Louisville, Ky.: Westminster/John Knox Press, 1991), 124.

18. Ibid., 127.

19. Italics mine. Karl Barth, *The Preaching of the Gospel*, trans. B. E. Hooke (Philadelphia: Westminster Press, 1963), 43. Also see Karl Barth, *Homiletics*, 76.

20. Barth, *Homiletics*, 76.

21. Jack Forstman traces Barth's stand regarding the rise of the Nazi state in an insightful book, *Christian Faith in Dark Times: Theological Conflicts in the Shadow of Hitler* (Louisville, Ky.: Westminster/John Knox Press, 1992), 255–59. Ultimately Barth failed, he concludes, because he believed "as a first act of faith that one accept the Bible as God's Word and that one assert this belief with no grounding that could be acknowledged from the outside." Because outsiders "do not share the premise, they understand themselves to be exempt from the claim of God to whom the

Bible witnesses." So Forstman regards Barth's "provincialism" with regard to the Bible as politically isolating—"one is limited to one's own enclave."

22. Barth, *Homiletics*, 118.

23. Barth, *Homiletics*, 118–19.

24. Barth, *Homiletics*, 119.

25. See my argument in "Preaching in an *Un*brave New World," *The Spire* (Vanderbilt Divinity School), 13, no. 1 (Summer/Fall 1988).

26. On the concept of "Just War," see Michael Walzer, *Just and Unjust Wars: A Moral Argument with Historical Illustrations*, 2d ed. (New York: Basic Books, 1992).

27. James Barr, "Revelation Through History in the Old Testament and in Modern Theology," in Martin E. Marty and Dean G. Peerman, eds., *New Theology No. 1* (New York: Macmillan Co., 1964), 60–74.

28. The phrase "salvation history" is, of course, a translation of the German *Heilsgeschichte*. The idea of a *Heilsgeschichte* is particularly associated with the thought of scholars such as Otto Piper, Oscar Cullmann, Paul Minear, and Jewish scholar Will Herberg.

29. The most penetrating "archaeology" of the scripture principle as well as the odd notion of "salvation history" is Edward Farley's *Ecclesial Reflection* (Philadelphia: Fortress Press, 1982), part 1.

30. For example, see Thomas G. Long's interesting apologetic for Revelation 15 and 16, "Praying for the Wrath of God," in *Preaching Through the Apocalypse*, ed. Cornish R. Rogers and Joseph R. Jeter, Jr. (St. Louis: Chalice Press, 1992), 133–39.

31. An argument I have ventured in my *Homiletic* (Philadelphia: Fortress Press, 1987), 239–50, with particular reference to Paul's discussion of authority in 1 Corinthians 1.

32. Philip Rieff, *The Triumph of the Therapeutic: Uses of Faith after Freud* (New York: Harper & Row, 1966).

33. The *Chicago Statement on Biblical Inerrancy* is explicit: "We deny that biblical infallibility and inerrancy are limited to spiritual, religious, or redemptive themes, exclusive of assertions in the fields of history and science. We further deny that scientific hypotheses about earth history may properly be used to overturn the teaching of scripture on creation and the flood." *Journal of the Evangelical Theological Society* 21 (1978): 289–96. Was it not H. L. Mencken who, referring to American fundamentalists, remarked,

"They are everywhere where learning is too heavy a burden for mortal minds to carry"?

34. Nineteenth-century British thought accepted scientific truth by verification, but seemed to affirm another mode of truth by intuition, a truth conveyed by poets, artists, and religious people. For various reasons, Americans did not embrace such a distinction easily. Thus, there have been sharp controversies in America between a rising scientific reading of reality and an embattled Bible Belt mentality—God's truth must be objectively true in all aspects of life. But prior to the emergence of the fundamentalist movement, Darwin's *Origin of the Species* (1859) agitated conservative Christians; see Harold Miller, "The Voice of God: Natural or Supernatural," *Preaching in American History. Selected Issues in the American Pulpit,* ed. DeWitte Holland (Nashville: Abingdon Press, 1969), 206–22.

35. On Spinoza, see Robert M. Grant and David Tracy, *A Short History of the Interpretation of the Bible,* 2d ed. (Philadelphia: Fortress Press, 1984), chap. 11.

36. See Harold Bloom, *The American Religion: The Emergence of the Post-Christian Nation* (New York: Simon & Schuster, 1992), chap. 2, "Enthusiasm, Gnosticism, American Orphism," and Robert N. Bellah et al., *Habits of the Heart: Individualism and Commitment in American Life* (Berkeley, Calif.: University of California Press, 1985).

37. The failure of the short-lived "New Hermeneutic" was because it understood scripture as addressed to an existential self in self-awareness and, following Heidegger, was leery of social language. (See Paul J. Achtemeier, *An Introduction to the New Hermeneutic* [Philadelphia: Westminster Press, 1969].) But, for the most part, the scriptures were written to the shared consciousness of religious communities.

38. For a useful presentation of "Critical Theory," see David Held, *Introduction to Critical Theory: Horkheimer to Habermas* (Berkeley, Calif.: University of California Press, 1980).

39. For some examples of the hermeneutic discussion, see J. S. Croatt, "Biblical Hermeneutics in the Theologies of Liberation," *Irruption of the Third World: Challenge to Theology,* ed. V. Fabella and S. Torres (Maryknoll, N.Y.: Orbis Books, 1983), 140–68; Elisabeth Schüssler Fiorenza, *Bread Not Stone: The Challenge of Feminist Biblical Interpretation* (Boston: Beacon Press, 1984), and *But She Said: Feminist Practices of Biblical Interpretation* (Boston: Beacon Press, 1992), as well as her article "Feminist Hermeneutics" in the *Anchor*

Bible Dictionary, ed. David Noel Freedman (Garden City, N.Y.: Doubleday & Co., 1992), 2:783–91; Justo L. González, *Out of Every Tribe and Nation: Christian Theology at the Ethnic Roundtable* (Nashville: Abingdon Press, 1992); Warren H. Stewart, Sr., *Interpreting God's Word in Black Preaching* (Valley Forge, Pa.: Judson Press, 1984).

40. See my essay "Preaching, Hermeneutics, and Liberation," in Paul P. Parker, ed., *Standing with the Poor: Theological Reflections on Economic Reality* (Cleveland: Pilgrim Press, 1992), 95–107.

41. See a remarkable chapter, "On Hearing the Gospel," in Joseph Haroutunian, *God with Us: A Theology of Transpersonal Life* (Philadelphia: Westminster Press, 1965), 175–98.

42. Buttrick, *Homiletic,* chap. 14.

43. Langdon Gilkey reports a survey of biblical knowledge in mainline churches and observes that "for all practical purposes the Bible is an unknown book to our congregations . . ."; see *How the Church Can Minister to the World without Losing Itself* (New York: Harper & Row, 1964), 86, n. 9.

44. On evangelism as a "fishing trip," see the remarkable study by Wilhelm H. Wuellner, *The Meaning of "Fishers of Men"* (Philadelphia: Westminster Press, 1967).

45. So, e.g., Andrew W. Blackwood in *The Preparation of Sermons* (Nashville: Abingdon Press, 1948) observed: "As a rule give the preference to *the short text.* In the sermon the minister can repeat a short text often, and the [layperson] can remember it easily. . . . Look at these texts . . . 'Choose life'; 'I will fear no evil: for thou art with me'; 'This is the way, walk ye in it'" (p. 50). Also see Ilion T. Jones *Principles and Practice of Preaching: A Comprehensive Study of the Art of Sermon Construction* (Nashville: Abingdon Press, 1956). Jones wrote: *"Use 'textual' sermons sparingly. . . .* In a textual sermon the points of the discussion are found in the text itself. . . . Mic. 6:8, 'He has showed you, O man, what is good; and what does the Lord require of you but to do justice, and to love kindness, and to walk humbly with your God?' is an example of a text that lends itself naturally to the 'textual' treatment. It states clearly three things that may become the three points of the outline. . . . Someone has estimated that it would be difficult, however, to find in the whole Bible a hundred texts suitable for textual treatment" (pp. 82–83). For a critique, see my "Preaching and Interpretation," *Interpretation* 35, no. 1 (January 1981): 46–58.

46. Such an assumption is not surprising in fundamentalism, but, unacknowledged, it may also be found in more liberal interpreters who seek to intuit general "truths" from religious writings.

Notes

47. Stanley Hauerwas and William H. Willimon, *Resident Aliens: A Provocative Christian Assessment of Culture and Ministry for People Who Know That Something Is Wrong* (Nashville: Abingdon Press, 1989); George Lindbeck, *The Nature of Doctrine: Religion and Theology in a Postliberal Age* (Philadelphia: Westminster Press, 1984). See an introductory essay in Stanley Hauerwas and L. Gregory Jones, eds., *Why Narrative? Readings in Narrative Theology* (Grand Rapids: Eerdmans, 1989).

48. Incidentally, as Letty Russell argues in *Household of Freedom: Authority in Feminist Theology* (Philadelphia: Westminster Press, 1987), without the end vision of the Bible we may have no basis for criticizing the Bible's own sexism, anti-Semitism, and military imagery.

49. Erich Auerbach, *Mimesis,* trans. Willard Trask (Princeton, N.J.: Princeton University Press, 1953). For a more recent treatment, see Robert Alter, *The Art of Biblical Narrative* (New York: Basic Books, 1981), and also an amazing work by Robert W. Funk, *The Poetics of Biblical Narrative* (Sonoma, Calif.: Polebridge Press, 1988).

50. We must not embrace the Hebrew Bible merely on the basis of christological reference, a practice to be found in the Protestant Reformers and more recently in scholars such as Wilhelm Vischer. The Hebrew scriptures offer structures of meaning in which we live—creation, eschaton, and the realization that events of our lives are also, at the same time, events in God's life with humanity. Yes, Jesus Christ is the central Christian symbol, but he appears as a character *in* Israel's story as much as, in retrospect, he may be the raison d'être for Israel's story. We Christians need not be imperialistic.

51. John Donahue, "Jesus as the Parable of God in the Gospel of Mark," *Interpretation* 32 (1978): 369–86; Edward Schillebeeckx, *Jesus* (New York: Crossroad, 1981), 158, 170.

52. I have written previously on narrative and meaning in *Homiletic,* 5–20; and also in *Preaching Jesus Christ* (Philadelphia: Fortress Press, 1988), chap. 6.

53. Thomas J. Talley, *The Origins of the Christian Year* (New York: Pueblo Publishing Co., 1986), 4, 13, 163, 231, 233, 235.

54. For a historical study, see John Reumann, "A History of Lectionaries: From the Synagogue at Nazareth to Post-Vatican II," *Interpretation* 31, no. 2 (April 1977): 116–30. For critical perspectives, in the same issue of *Interpretation,* see Lloyd R. Bailey, "The Lectionary in Critical Perspective," 139–53; also see Shelly E.

Cochran, "The Church Year and Its Influence on Preaching," *The Academy of Homiletics: Papers of the Annual Meeting* (December 4–8, 1990), 33–42. Dr. Cochran spots "inherent biases and hermeneutic tendencies" in a very savvy fashion.

55. George Herbert Mead, *Mind, Self, and Society from the Standpoint of a Social Behaviorist* (Chicago: University of Chicago Press, 1934).

56. See the important Gifford Lectures by James Barr, *Biblical Faith and Natural Theology* (Oxford: Clarendon Press, 1993).

57. The phrase "disclosure model" is Ian T. Ramsey's. For an initial definition, see his *Models and Mystery* (London: Oxford University Press, 1964), 9–10. He too uses the term with reference to Jesus Christ: "There was discerned in Jesus that same individuation which was disclosed in and through the universe. In other words, it was as and when a cosmic disclosure occurred around him . . . that men spoke and have spoken of the activity of God" (*Models for Divine Activity* [London: SCM Press, 1973], 40).

58. Friedrich Nietzsche, *Thus Spoke Zarathustra, in The Portable Nietzsche*, ed. Walter Kaufmann (New York: Viking Press, 1954), 375–79.

59. Friedrich Schleiermacher, *On Religion: Speeches to Its Cultured Despisers*, trans. Richard Crouter (New York: Cambridge University Press, 1988), 135. For Schleiermacher on scriptural authority, see Robert Clyde Johnson, *Authority in Protestant Theology* (Philadelphia: Westminster Press, 1959), 64–74.

60. Augustine said much the same thing: "Thus a man supported by faith, hope, and charity, with an unshaken hold upon them, does not need the Scripture except for the instruction of others," *On Christian Doctrine* (1.39.43) trans. D. W. Robertson, Jr. (Indianapolis: Bobbs-Merrill Co., 1958), 32.

61. *The New Schaff-Herzog Encyclopedia of Religious Knowledge* (ed. S. M. Jackson [Grand Rapids: Baker Book House, 1953], 12:421. Cited in Walter R. Wietzke, *The Primacy of the Spoken Word: Redemptive Proclamation in a Complex World* (Minneapolis: Augsburg Publishing House, 1988), 32.

62. WA 12:259; WA 10, I, 1, 17; cited with discussion in Willem Jan Kooiman, *Luther and the Bible* (Philadelphia: Muhlenberg Press, 1961), 201.

63. Calvin, born in 1509, published his first book in 1532 at the ripe young age of 22. A whiz kid indeed!

64. *Calvini Opera—Corpus Reformatorum* 53.266.15–30, quoted

in T.H.L. Parker, *Calvin's Preaching* (Louisville, Ky.: Westminster/John Knox Press, 1992), 24.

65. See my article on Reformed Liturgy in Donald K. McKim, ed., *Encylopedia of the Reformed Faith* (Louisville, Ky.: Westminster/John Knox Press, 1992), 220–23.

66. Calvin, *Institutes*, 1.9.3.

67. Second Helvetic Confession (1566), I. Text from Arthur C. Cochrane, *Reformed Confessions of the 16th Century* (Philadelphia: Westminster Press, 1965).

68. Thomas Aquinas, *Summa Theologica*. Trans. Fathers of the English Dominican Province. 3 vols. (New York: Benzinger Brothers, 1947–48, I, Q. 1, art. 109, ad 1 [1.7].

69. *Rome and the Study of Scripture* (7th ed.), ed. Conrad Lewis, O.S.B. (St. Meinrad, Ind.: Abbey Press, 1964), 24. See also a discussion of issues in Karl Rahner, *Inspiration in the Bible* (New York: Herder & Herder, 1964).

70. On scripture and tradition, see George H. Tavard, *Holy Writ or Holy Church* (London: Burns & Oates, 1959); Karl Rahner and Joseph Ratzinger, *Revelation and Tradition* (New York: Herder & Herder, 1966); Yves Congar, O.P., *Tradition and Traditions* (London: Burns & Oates, 1966). For a Protestant discussion of the Catholic position, see Donald K. McKim, *What Christians Believe about the Bible* (Nashville: Thomas Nelson, 1985), 9–23.

71. Reinhold Seeberg, *Text-book of the History of Doctrines*, vol. 2, trans. Charles E. Hay (Grand Rapids: Baker Book House, 1966), §71, 2.

72. James Barr, "Biblical Scholarship and the Unity of the Church," *Nineteenth Lecture of the Robinson T. Orr Visitorship* (London, Ont.: Huron College, 1989), 14.

73. The Reformers' position on the authority of the Bible is modified by their insistence on the inner testimony of the Spirit in the hearing/interpretation of scripture. But the duality of their position—Word and Spirit—has become trapped in the thought forms of Enlightenment, i.e., objective and subjective. Thus, in our age, the "subjective/objective split" threatens the basic theological construct of Protestantism.

74. WA 40, part 1, 600.13.

75. B. A. Gerrish, *The Old Protestantism and the New: Essays on the Reformation Heritage* (Chicago: University of Chicago Press, 1982), 55.

76. Philip S. Watson, *Let God Be God: An Interpretation of the Theology of Martin Luther* (Philadelphia: Fortress Press, 1947), 175.

77. From *Calvin's Commentaries*, ed. Joseph Haroutunian, Library of Christian Classics (Philadelphia: Westminster Press, 1958), 70; quoted in B. A. Gerrish, *The Old Protestantism*, 61.

78. In my *Homiletic*, chap. 15, I have argued that Paul's authority is Christ crucified, recalled in consciousness as a saving message. In other words, though Paul is familiar with both scripture and tradition and, in other contexts, will appeal to both, his ultimate authority appears to be the foolish, impotency of the cross. Though Reformers set scripture over against papacy and tradition, nevertheless their primary concern is also with the liberating message of Jesus Christ crucified. But in the subsequent Reformed tradition, some ideas of biblical authority are based on God's monarchical domination which, of course, is antithetical to God revealed in the helplessness of Christ crucified. Scripture should be aligned by incarnational analogy with the loving weakness of *crucified* Christ.

79. LW 35:123. As quoted in Paul D. L. Alvis, *The Church in the Theology of the Reformers* (Atlanta: John Knox Press, 1981), 83.

80. LW 54:394f. Quoted in Alvis, *The Church,* 81.

81. CO 24:453. Quoted in Alvis, *The Church,* 83. Calvin believes that we must *hear* the message of the scriptures. So he attacks "fanatical men" who suppose they can profit from "private reading and meditation" and "deem preaching superfluous." No, "[God] also provides for our weakness in that [God] prefers to address us in human fashion through interpreters in order to draw us . . . rather than to thunder at us and drive us away." *Institutes* 4.1.5.

82. B. A. Gerrish, *The Old Protestantism,* 63.

83. *Homilies on I Samuel*, 42 (CR 39: 705).

84. Calvin, *Institutes*, 4.1.5.

85. 1 Tim. 5:20. Sermon 43, CO 53:520. See discussion in T.H.L. Parker, *Calvin's Preaching,* 35–47.

86. Calvin, like Luther, comes close to defining a canon within the canon. In *Institutes,* 3.2.6–7, Calvin says that faith rests on the promises of God. Apparently, Pighius criticized Calvin for saying that faith is especially based on the promises: Did Calvin suggest that faith was not related to *all* the words of God? For discussion, see B. A. Gerrish, *The Old Protestantism,* 62.

87. Edward A. Dowey, Jr., observes the same unresolved tension in Calvin's thought; see *The Knowledge of God in Calvin's Theology* (New York: Columbia University Press, 1952, reprinted 1966), 160ff. H. J. Forstman arrives at a similar conclusion in *Word*

and Spirit: Calvin's Doctrine of Biblical Authority (Stanford, Calif.: Stanford University Press, 1962).

88. Fred B. Craddock, *As One without Authority: Essays on Inductive Preaching* (Nashville: Abingdon Press, 1978).

89. John R. Fry's *The Great Apostolic Blunder Machine: A Contemporary Attack upon Christendom* (San Francisco: Harper & Row, 1978) is still an important book and probably should be required reading for prospective clergy.

90. A thesis ventured persuasively by Marshall McLuhan, particularly in *The Gutenberg Galaxy: The Making of Typographic Man* (Toronto: University of Toronto Press, 1962). The thesis is developed further in the many works of Walter J. Ong, S.J., for example, *Interfaces of the Word: Studies in the Evolution of Consciousness and Culture* (New York: Cornell University Press, 1977) and *The Presence of the Word: Some Prolegomena for Cultural and Religious History* (New Haven, Conn.: Yale University Press, 1967). See also Frederick E. Crowe, S.J., *Theology of the Christian Word: A Study in History* (New York: Paulist Press, 1978).

91. Neil Postman, *Amusing Ourselves to Death: Public Discourse in the Age of Show Business* (New York: Viking Penguin, 1985), part 1.

Chapter 2. Preaching and Church

1. In Greek, *romphaia;* the word is also used in the Septuagint at Isa. 11:4 and 49:2; in Wisd. of Sol. 18:15; *1 Enoch* 62:2; and *2 Esdras* [*4 Ezra*] 13:10. In the Christian scriptures, see 2 Thess. 2:8; Heb. 4:12; and Eph. 6:17.

2. I have written on resurrection passages in "Preaching on the Resurrection," *Religion in Life* 45, no. 3 (Autumn 1976): 278–95; *Preaching Jesus Christ* (Philadelphia: Fortress Press, 1988), 57–68; and, most recently, *The Mystery and the Passion: A Homiletic Reading of the Gospel Traditions* (Minneapolis: Fortress Press, 1992), 15–91.

3. Willi Marxsen, *The Resurrection of Jesus of Nazareth* (Philadelphia: Fortress Press, 1970).

4. Matt. 28:16–20. For an important discussion of the passage, see Douglas R. A. Hare, *Matthew* (Louisville, Ky: John Knox Press, 1993), 331–35.

5. Luke 24:47. Notice that Paul also links resurrection and the forgiveness of sins; see 1 Cor. 15:17.

6. The number of disciples dispatched is, of course, a Lukan addition [see Matt. 9:37–38 and Luke 10:1]. In Luke the 70 [or 72]

correspond to the supposed number of nations in Genesis 10. Luke sees Christianity in worldwide evangelical mission. For discussion of the peculiar passage in Luke, see Charles H. Talbert, *Reading Luke: A Literary and Theological Commentary on the Third Gospel* (New York: Crossroad, 1986), 114–19; also, see a chapter by Paul S. Minear, "The Source of Authority," *To Heal and Reveal: The Prophetic Vocation according to Luke* (New York: Seabury Press, 1976), 3–30.

7. See 1 Cor. 15:17; Mark 16:5–8; Matt. 28:16–20; Luke 24:13–47; John 20:19–23; 21:1–14.

8. Despite the sharp division drawn between preaching and teaching by C. H. Dodd in *The Apostolic Preaching and Its Developments* (New York: Harper & Brothers, 1949), the Christian scriptures do not limit preaching to kerygmatic proclamation alone. Preaching can console, teach, exhort, as well as declare *kerygma*.

9. Luke 24:25–27; see also, my "Homiletic Resources for the Easter Season," *Quarterly Review* 6, no. 1 (Spring 1986): 65–85.

10. See Robert H. Smith, *Easter Gospels: The Resurrection of Jesus according to the Four Evangelists* (Minneapolis: Augsburg Publishing House, 1983), 34–35. In an extensive footnote, Smith reviews scholarly interpretations of the young man that have been ventured; 225–26, n. 43.

11. See D. Buttrick, *Easter, Proclamation 5: Series A* (Minneapolis: Fortress Press, 1993), 14–16; idem, *The Mystery*, 87–88.

12. Calvin: *Institutes*, 1.7.4; 4.8.8. On Luther, see Regin Prenter, *Spiritus Creator*, trans. John M. Jensen (Philadelphia: Muhlenberg Press, 1953), 101–30.

13. *Calvin: Institutes*, 1.7.4. For Luther, see Prenter, *Spiritus*, 102f., 122f.

14. LW 42:59. Cited in Walter R. Wietzke, *The Primacy of the Spoken Word*, 32.

15. *akoas pisteos*, in Gal. 3:2, is hard to translate—faith-hearing, hearing faithfully, hearing with faith. Hans Dieter Betz renders the phrase "proclamation of [the] faith," and argues that the phrase "shifts the emphasis from hearing to the preaching of the message." (*Galatians* [Philadelphia: Fortress Press, 1979], 128).

16. See Luther's *That Jesus Christ Was Born a Jew*, LW 45; but also, in a more polemic mood, his *On the Jews and Their Lies*, LW 47; and, against both Jews and Muslims, *On the Last Words of David*, LW 15. Luther did encourage a translation of the Koran into Latin, albeit to provide fodder for polemic attack; see Paul D. L. Avis, *The Church in the Theology of the Reformers* (Atlanta: John Knox Press,

1981), 208. Luther's anti-Semitism is well known. Calvin's treatment of Christianity and the Jews is primarily limited to his commentary on Rom. 9—11.

17. Cited by Philip S. Watson, *Let God Be God*, 168; but see also subsequent discussion, 168–72. Watson takes pains to refute John Wesley's famous verdict: "Who has wrote more ably than Martin Luther on justification by faith alone?" Wesley observed, "and who was more ignorant of the doctrine of sanctification . . . ?"

18. For discussion of Luther and Calvin on justification and sanctification, see Wilhelm Niesel, *The Gospel and the Churches: A Comparison of Catholicism, Orthodoxy, and Protestantism*, trans. David Lewis (Philadelphia: Westminster Press, 1962), 191–200.

19. *Institutes* 4.3.1.

20. *Institutes* 4.8.4.

21. *Institutes* 4.8.2.

22. On Deut. 1:17. CO 25: 647ff. Cited in T.H.L. Parker, *Calvin's Preaching*, 26.

23. Cited by Parker, *Calvin's Preaching*, 14.

24. *Institutes* 3.4.14.

25. LW 40. 37. Cited in Avis, *The Church*, 20.

26. WA 1:113, 4ff. Cited in Watson, *Let God Be God*, 181, n. 69. For contemporary discussion, see Gerhard O. Forde, *Theology Is for Proclamation* (Minneapolis: Fortress Press, 1990). Forde builds a theology on Luther's distinction "between God not preached and God preached."

27. LW 54:317f.

28. Langdon Gilkey, *How the Church Can Minister to the World without Losing Itself*, 84.

29. "Truth through personality" is a phrase associated with Phillips Brooks, *Lectures on Preaching* (New York: E. P. Dutton, 1902), 5. Brooks wrote, "What, then, is preaching, of which we are to speak? It is not hard to find a definition. Preaching is the communication of truth by man to men [*sic*]. It has in it two essential elements, truth and personality. Neither of those can it spare and still be preaching." The featured, lighted pulpit came along not merely to enhance solo evangelists but, oddly enough, showed up with the "Gothic revival" of worship in the 1920s.

30. See a brilliant but neglected book by Theodore W. Jennings, Jr., *Life as Worship: Prayer and Praise in Jesus' Name* (Grand Rapids: Eerdmans, 1982).

31. B. A. Gerrish states that Protestant Reformers saw worship as gratitude: "Worship, according to the Reformers, consists

chiefly in gratitude, its goal is the honoring of God's name, and its form is eucharistic."; see, "The Reformers' Theology of Worship," *McCormick Quarterly* 14, no. 4 (May 1961): 21–29.

32. The title of a book on worship by Marianne H. Micks, *The Future Present: The Phenomenon of Christian Worship* (New York: The Seabury Press, 1970).

33. The phrase presence-in-absence is borrowed from Jean-Paul Sartre, and I use the phrase intending his phenomenology of time, memory, anticipation, and presence, a phenomenology woven into his *Being and Nothingness* (New York: Philosophical Library, 1956). The use of Sartre's categories was suggested to me long ago by a chapter, "Christ and Worship," in Roger Hazelton, *Christ and Ourselves: A Clue to Christian Life Today* (New York: Harper & Row, 1965), 71–95.

34. But see the analysis of Harnack by Wilhelm Pauck, *Harnack and Troeltsch: Two Historical Theologians* (New York: Oxford University Press, 1968).

35. Many free churches that seldom celebrate the Lord's Supper seem to turn toward moral regulation. But at least they realize that Christian people should model the gospel message. Mainline Christianity may be too easy.

36. The argument in this paragraph draws on my essay, "A Sketchbook: Preaching and Worship," LeRoy E. Kennel, ed., *Preaching and Worship* (Princeton, N.J.: Academy of Homiletics, 1980): 5–12.

37. Barth, Homiletics, 58–59.

38. If Christ is both the word we preach and the real presence of eucharist, then there is no need to build "mood bridges," even when Christ's word speaks judgment. In eucharist, we celebrate the sure promise of our reconciliation in Christ, but if we are divided and contentious, we will eat and drink judgment on ourselves. Remember, according to Paul, the Lord's Supper in Corinth had become a judgment.

39. Charles L. Rice, a fine homiletician who has written a fine book, slides toward such a position in *The Embodied Word: Preaching as Art and Liturgy* (Minneapolis: Fortress Press, 1991), 49–70.

40. *leitourgia* means a public work of the people and may imply some sense of obligation; we owe God *leitourgia*. For a brief discussion, see Adolf Adam, *Foundations of Liturgy: An Introduction to Its History and Practice* (Collegeville: Liturgical Press, 1992), 3–4.

41. The tension is acknowledged by J.-J. von Allmen, *Worship: Its*

Theology and Practice (New York: Oxford University Press, 1965); see also a somewhat singular article by Steven Franklin, "The Primacy of Preaching," *Covenant Quarterly* 48, no. 1 (1990): 3–37.

42. Charles Rice (*The Embodied Word*, 127) quotes Joseph Sittler: "Preaching is an act of the church in which the substance of her faith is ever freshly declared . . . " (*The Anguish of Preaching* [Philadelphia: Fortress Press, 1966], 7). But in the same book (p. 30), Sittler, who was not only a super theologian but a sturdy Lutheran, wrote of the anguish preachers know because their word must be Christ's word: "One is never a successful preacher; one is never a successful teacher—if the matter of [one's] work be Christ. How one hopes, works to come to terms with the anguish that runs forever deeply under the incomplete and faltering efforts that one makes! And how incessant and beguiling the temptation to *settle* for . . ."I have done what I can—let me now have pity on myself and be joyful"! But just as one thinks [one]self on the way to a "professional" aplomb as a preacher or teacher, the figure of Jesus, expanded, made present, and urgent by the entire Christology that ceaselessly flows out from him—that figure turns, as he did to pathetic Peter in the courtyard. And under that look everything is crumpled save the presence and the question and the anguish." We are called to ministry by Christ through the voice of the church, but not by church alone.

43. LW 48:112, 364–72. Luther recommends a second question. The *Schwärmer* should be asked about Christian experience. If they describe their life in Christ as "pleasant, quiet, and devout," then Luther urges Melanchthon to reject them as charlatans. On Luther's view of ministry, see B. A. Gerrish, "Priesthood and Ministry: Luther's Fifth Means of Grace," *The Old Protestantism*, 90–105.

44. See, e.g., Lyle Schaller, *Effective Church Planning* (Nashville: Abingdon Press, 1979); *Reflections of a Contrarian: Second Thoughts on the Parish Ministry* (Nashville: Abingdon Press, 1989); and many others.

45. Gary B. Trudeau's "Doonesbury," Sunday, June 27, 1993.

46. Some years ago, Douglas John Hall wrote a careful indictment of mainline "establishment" Christianity, *The Reality of the Gospel and the Unreality of the Churches* (Philadelphia: Westminster Press, 1975). The book is still helpful reading.

47. For example, James E. Means, *Leadership in Christian Ministry* (Grand Rapids: Baker Book House, 1989), 57–69; for a critique see Carnegie S. Calian, *Today's Pastor in Tomorrow's World* (Philadelphia:

Westminster Press, 1982), 32f. Though the term "enabler" is seldom used in more recent literature, the concept lingers.

48. Edward Farley, "Praxis and Piety: Hermeneutics beyond the New Dualism," *Justice and the Holy: Essays in Honor of Walter Harrelson*, ed. Douglas A. Knight and Peter J. Paris (Atlanta: Scholars Press, 1989), 247.

49. The idea of a Word-of-God Bible, on the one hand, and a congregation permanently endowed with the Spirit, on the other, is not far from a model we find in the thought of Ulrich Zwingli. See *Zwingli and Bullinger*, ed. G. W. Bromiley (Philadelphia: Westminster Press, 1953), 31–40.

50. Has preaching become linked to the well-being of the church because of a Pauline notion? In 1 Cor. 14:5 and 14:12, Paul sets a criterion for speaking in church, namely, upbuilding the congregation. But Paul is referring to charismatic tongues and how to judge their worth. Certainly, upbuilding the church is not the sole purpose of preaching. For Paul, preaching is connected with God's redemptive purpose for the whole human world. Moreover, upbuilding a church to Paul does *not* mean numerical strength or positive "vibes."

51. For analysis of the religious scene since the 1950s, see Robert Wuthnow, *The Restructuring of American Religion: Society and Faith since World War II* (Princeton, N.J.: Princeton University Press, 1988). There is a shibboleth to the effect that mainline denominations have faltered because they are liberal and that, by contrast, conservative churches are multiplying. Long ago I was helped by Eugene A. Nida, an ace religious sociologist, who seemed to establish that churches grow by preaching to the poor; see *Message and Mission*, chap. 5. In the 1950s, mainline Protestant denominations, following cash, moved to the suburbs, and decline was inevitable.

52. I have been unable to locate and date the cartoon.

53. Stanley Hauerwas and William H. Willimon, *Resident Aliens: A Provocative Christian Assessment of Culture and Ministry for People Who Know That Something Is Wrong* (Nashville: Abingdon Press, 1989); Hauerwas and Willimon, "Why *Resident Aliens* Struck a Chord," *Missiology* 19 (1991): 419–29; Hauerwas, *After Christendom?* (Nashville: Abingdon Press, 1991).

54. Is there any greater terror than an absence of the Word of God? T. S. Eliot catches the mood:

> Will you leave my people forgetful and forgotten
> To idleness, labour, and delirious stupor?

There shall be left the broken chimney,
The peeled hull, a pile of rusty iron,
In a street of scattered brick where the goat climbs,
Where My Word is unspoken. . . .

Where My Word is unspoken,
In the land of the lobelias and tennis flannels
The rabbit shall burrow and the thorn revisit,
The nettle shall flourish on the gravel court,
And the wind shall say: "Here were decent godless people:
Their only monument the asphalt road
And a thousand lost golf balls."

"Choruses from 'The Rock,'" *Collected Poems 1909–1935* (New York: Harcourt, Brace & Company, 1936), 190.

55. In the 1930s, Barth established theological method in a book on Anselm (*Anselm: Fides quaerens intellectum* [Richmond: John Knox Press, 1960]). Since then, Barth's focus has been on God's biblical self-communication to the *faith* of the church.

56. Once, mainline churches addressed the wider social world and were concerned with cultural thought, e.g., Julian N. Hartt, *A Christian Critique of American Culture: An Essay in Practical Theology* (New York: Harper & Row, 1967). Of late, apologetic literature has been produced largely by conservative Christian groups; for example, a perceptive study by William A. Dyrness, *How Does America Hear the Gospel?* (Grand Rapids: Eerdmans, 1989). But apologetics should always be a homiletic concern; see Avery Dulles, *A History of Apologetics* (Philadelphia: Westminster Press, 1971).

57. Obviously, the recent hoopla over "narrative preaching" is a symptom of a cultural shift from vertical to horizontal structures of meaning. Process theology and liberation theology likewise employ horizontal models. The Bible, however, contains both models: So-called "coronation psalms" bear witness to Yahweh's "vertical" kingship, but Yahweh is also a traveler: "Thus says the Lord: Are you the one to build me a house to live in? I have not lived in a house since the day when I brought up the people of Israel from Egypt to this day, but I have been moving about . . ." (2 Sam. 7:5b–6).

58. Frank Kermode, *The Sense of an Ending: Studies in the Theory of Fiction* (New York: Oxford University Press, 1967).

59. Roi Ottley, *New World a-Coming* (New York: Arno Press [1943] 1968).

60. For example, see novels of Walker Percy such as *Love in the Ruins* (1971); the less successful *Lancelot* (1977) ; and a truly wonderful book, *The Second Coming* (1980).

61. Jeremiah 7:1–15. As temple-goers, the people of Judah felt protected from the judgment of God. Over and over they recited their religious conviction: "This is the temple of the Lord, the temple of the Lord, the temple of the Lord, the temple of the Lord."

Chapter 3. Preaching and Culture

1. I am drawing on a literature that might be labeled "Christianinity *and* culture." Of late, such literature has dwindled, perhaps because of the odd cultural isolation of Christian communities. But from the 1940s through the 1960s many books were written, for example: Emil Brunner, *The Word of God and Modern Man* (1947); *Christianity and Civilization* (1949); Christopher Dawson, *Religion and Culture* (1948); T. S. Eliot, *Notes toward the Definition of Culture* (1949); H. Richard Niebuhr, *Christ and Culture* (1951); Richard Kroner, *Culture and Faith* (1951); Paul Tillich, *The Religious Situation* (1932); *The Protestant Era* (1948); *Theology of Culture* (1959); books by Denis de Rougement, *Man's Western Quest* (1957); *The Christian Opportunity* (1963); works by Bernard Meland, *Faith and Culture* (1955); *Fallible Forms and Symbols* (1976); Julian N. Hartt, *A Christian Critique of American Culture* (1967); Harvey Cox, *The Secular City* (1965); and many works by Jacques Ellul, *The Technological Society* (1964); *The Political Illusion* (1967); *The Meaning of the City* (1970); *The Humiliation of the Word* (1985). For an overview, see Edward Cell, ed., *Religion and Contemporary Western Culture: Selected Readings* (Nashville: Abingdon Press, 1967).

2. The discussion goes all the way back to Auguste Comte. For positions, see essays in Gloria B. Levitas, *Culture and Consciousness: Perspectives in the Social Sciences* (New York: George Braziller, 1967.

3. Crane Brinton, *A History of Western Morals* (New York: Harcourt, Brace & Co., 1959), introduction.

4. Harper Lee, *To Kill a Mockingbird* (New York: Popular Library, 1962), 284.

5. For a perceptive analysis of the problem, see Stephen Sykes, *The Identity of Christianity: Theologians and the Essence of Christianity from Schleiermacher to Barth* (Philadelphia: Fortress Press, 1984).

6. Though the biblical theology movement supposed a basic

unity of the biblical message (e.g., H. H. Rowley, *The Unity of the Bible* [Philadelphia: Westminster Press, 1955]), few scholars would venture such a position now; for example, James D. G. Dunn, *Unity and Diversity in the New Testament: An Inquiry into the Character of Earliest Christianity* (Philadelphia: Westminster Press, 1977).

7. Denis de Rougemont, *Love in the Western World*, trans. Montgomery Belgion (Garden City, N.Y.: Doubleday & Co., 1957), book II.

8. See Gerard S. Sloyan, *The Jesus Tradition: Images of Jesus in the West* (Mystic, Conn.: Twenty-Third Publications, 1986); Irenee Noye et al., *Jesus in Christian Devotion and Contemplation* (St. Meinrad, Ind.: Abbey Press, 1974); J. Pelikan, *Jesus through the Centuries* (New Haven, Conn.: Yale University, 1985).

9. Conflict over a Gentile mission can be traced through the Christian scriptures; see Johannes Munck, *Paul and the Salvation of Mankind* (Richmond: John Knox Press, 1959), 87–134, 210–46, 247–81.

10. See Gerd Lüdemann, *Early Christianity according to the Traditions in Acts: A Commentary* (Minneapolis: Fortress Press, 1987).

11. Martin Hengel, *Judaism & Hellenism: Studies in Their Encounter in Palestine during the Early Hellenistic Period*, trans. John Bowden, 2 vols. (Philadelphia: Fortress Press, 1974), 1:105.

12. See George Steiner, *After Babel: Aspects of Language and Translation* (New York: Oxford University Press, 1975), in particular, chap. 1. Steiner also provides an extensive bibliography on the processes involved in translating, 475–84.

13. I have been unable to locate a source for the example. Eugene Nida gives several cases of translating the word "faith"—"hanging onto God with the heart,""to lean on God,""joining God's word to one's body"—in *Message and Mission*, 67.

14. Nida, *Message and Mission*, 194.

15. See F. W. Dillistone, *Christianity and Communication* (London: Collins, 1956), chap. 4; also see Jules L. Moreau, *Language and Religious Language* (Philadelphia: Westminster Press, 1961), chap. V.

16. Faith *must* employ figurative language—metaphors for God and metaphors to express the inwardness of faith. See Sallie McFague, *Metaphorical Theology: Models of God in Religious Language* (Philadelphia: Fortress Press, 1982). See also my discussion of preaching language in *Homiletic*, 113–25, 187–98.

17. Samuel Sandmel, *Philo of Alexandria: An Introduction* (New York: Oxford University Press, 1979), 89–101.

18. Allegory moves toward an equal sign between faith and culture. On allegory, see Edwin Honig, *Dark Conceit: The Making of Allegory* (New York: Oxford University Press, 1966).

19. In evangelical, missionary eras, the interpretation of faith is usually "Alexandrian." The most famous of the Alexandrians, Origen (c. 230 C.E.) recognized that scripture is literal/historical, but proposed "spiritual" meanings as well that permitted him to align the gospel to Greek thought.

20. Acts 17:16–34; see Robert C. Tannehill, *The Narrative Unity of Luke-Acts: A Literary Interpretation*, 2 vols. (Minneapolis: Fortress Press, 1986–90), 2:210–20.

21. André Grabar, *Early Christian Art: From the Rise of Christianity to the Death of Theodosius*, trans. Stuart Gilbert and James Emmens (New York: Odyssey Press, 1968), 80, 252–53; Robert Milburn, *Early Christian Art and Architecture* (Berkeley, Calif.: University of California Press, 1988), 176–77; Pierre du Bourguet, S.J., *Early Christian Painting*, trans. Simon Watson Taylor (New York: Viking Press, 1965), 14–17. For a general study, see Walter Lowrie, *Art in the Early Church* (New York: W. W. Norton & Co., 1947).

22. For example, "great is the mystery of our religion" (1 Tim. 3:16) parallels lines from a hymn to the many-breasted Diana of the Ephesians. On early Christian liturgical borrowing, see Anscar J. Chupungco, O.S.B., *Cultural Adaptation of the Liturgy* (New York: Paulist Press, 1982). On the general issue of cultural adaptation in liturgy, see Frank C. Senn, *Christian Worship and Its Cultural Setting* (Philadelphia: Fortress Press, 1983).

23. Brinton, *A History of Western Morals*, chaps. XI and XII.

24. D. H. Lawrence, *Lady Chatterley's Lover* (New York: The Modern Library, 1959).

25. Emil Brunner, *The Scandal of Christianity* (Philadelphia: Westminster Press, 1951).

26. Gen. 1:31. For discussion, see Claus Westermann, *Genesis 1—11: A Commentary*, trans. John J. Scullion, S.J. (Minneapolis: Augsburg Publishing House, 1982), 165–67.

27. Christian prudishness with regard to creaturely pleasures began early; see 1 Tim. 4:1–5.

28. For discussion, see Jaroslav Pelikan, *The Growth of Medieval Theology (600–1300)* (Chicago: University of Chicago Press, 1978), 293–307.

29. See Carl L. Becker, *The Heavenly City of the Eighteenth-Century Philosophers* (New Haven, Conn.: Yale University Press, 1932), chap. II.

30. Eugène Ionesco, *The Killer and Other Plays* (New York: Grove Press, 1960), 19. In the same speech, Bérenger complains ". . . when there's not a total agreement between myself inside and myself outside, then it's a catastrophe, a universal contradiction, a schism."

31. Job 14:14. The whole chapter is blunt; here is v. 1:

> A mortal, born of woman,
>> few of days and full of trouble,
> comes up like a flower and withers,
>> flees like a shadow and does not last.

32. The phrase may refer to the resurrection of the church, the body of Christ. For discussion, see John A. T. Robinson's monograph, *The Body: A Study in Pauline Theology* (London: SCM, 1963), chap. 3.

33. Gerhard Kittel and Gerhard Friedrich, eds., *Theological Dictionary of the New Testament*, 10 vols., trans. Geoffrey W. Bromiley (Grand Rapids: Eerdmans, 1964–76).

34. For a survey of positions on the "Image of God," see David Cairns, *The Image of God in Man* (London: Collins, 1973).

35. Theories of history are inevitable. See, Patrick Gardiner, ed., *Theories of History* (Glencoe, Ill.: Free Press, 1959), and Hans Meyerhoff, ed., *The Philosophy of History in Our Time* (New York: Garland Publishing, 1985).

36. For discussion of storied readings of history, see essays in W.J.T. Mitchell, *On Narrative* (Chicago: University of Chicago Press, 1981).

37. Kofi Awoonor, *The Breast of the Earth: A Survey of the History, Culture, and Literature of Africa South of the Sahara* (Garden City, N.Y.: Anchor Press, 1975); *African Culture: The Rhythms of Unity*, ed. Kete Asante Molefi and Kariamu Welshe Asante, *Contributions in Afro-American and African Studies*, No. 81 (Westport, Conn.: Greenwood Press, 1985); Chancellor Williams, *The Destruction of Black Civilization: Great Issues of a Race from 4500 B.C. to 2000 A.D.* (Chicago: Third World Press, 1987); for a general survey, Roland Oliver, *The African Experience* (New York: HarperCollins, 1991).

38. Many cultural historians pick out similar epochal periods —a Classical world, a medieval world, and an Enlightenment. For example, Paul Tillich, "The World Situation," in *The Christian Answer*, ed. Henry P. Van Dusen (New York: Charles Scribner's Sons, 1945), 1–44.

39. Arnold J. Toynbee, *A Study of History*, abridged by D. C. Somervell, 2 vols. (New York: Oxford University Press, 1946–57), 2:263–65, 307–09.

40. See Alfredo Fierro, *The Militant Gospel: A Critical Introduction to Political Theologies*, trans. John Drury (Maryknoll, N.Y.: Orbis Books, 1977), part I.

41. Leonardo Boff, *New Evangelization: Good News to the Poor*, trans. Robert R. Barr (Maryknoll, N.Y.: Orbis Books, 1991).

42. See Walbert Bühlmann, *The Coming of the Third Church: An Analysis of the Present and the Future of the Church* (Maryknoll, N.Y.: Orbis Books, 1982).

43. To spread subculturally, Christianity will need support from established churches. Churches ought to fund nonparish ministries within countercultural movements. But, in the United States, denominations are into self-preservation and dwindling funds are spent on established programs. As a result, mainline churches are discouraging nonparish ministries, even though they may have a clergy surplus. For discussion of theological issues, F. W. Dillistone, *Revelation and Evangelism* (London: Lutterworth Press, 1948), particularly chaps. 2 and 3.

44. Kim Yong Bock, ed., *Minjung Theology: People as the Subjects of History* (Singapore: The Commission on Theological Concerns, Christian Conference of Asia, 1981).

45. On metaphor and culture, see Philip Wheelwright, *Metaphor and Reality* (Bloomington, Ind.: Indiana University Press, 1968); also George Lakoff and Mark Johnson, *Metaphors We Live By* (Chicago: University of Chicago Press, 1980).

46. See Eric A. Havelock, *Reflections on Orality and Literacy from Antiquity to the Present* (New Haven, Conn.: Yale University Press, 1986); see also David Crystal, ed., *The Cambridge Encyclopedia of Language* (Cambridge: Cambridge University Press, 1987), part V.

47. McLuhan, *The Gutenberg Galaxy*; see also Walter J. Ong, S.J., *Orality and Literacy: The Technologizing of the Word* (London: Methuen & Co., 1982).

48. Peter L. Berger, *The Sacred Canopy: Elements of a Sociological Theory of Religion* (Garden City, N.Y.: Doubleday & Co., 1967), chaps. 1 and 2.

49. I have spelled "gods" with a lowercase "g." These are culturally defined "gods," namely, generally accepted moral values or even generally accepted notions of the sacred. Thus, though some critics consider Shakespeare a "Christian" dramatist, the "gods" in his tragedies are quite conventional.

50. David Tracy, *Blessed Rage for Order: The New Pluralism in Theology* (New York: Seabury Press, 1975), chap. 3.

51. See Paul M. van Buren, *The Edges of Language: An Essay in the Logic of Religion* (New York: Macmillan Co., 1972) for a helpful discussion of the language of faith in relation to "puns, poetry, and paradox."

52. From Wallace Stevens's "The Man with The Blue Guitar," xxxii in *Collected Poems of Wallace Stevens* (New York: Alfred A. Knopf, 1954), 183, as cited with italics by Stanley Hopper in "The Word as Symbol in Sacred Experience," *Silence, the Word, and the Sacred*, ed. E. D. Blodgett and H. G. Coward (Waterloo, Ont.: Wilfrid Laurier University Press, 1989), 83–109.

53. See Paul Scott Wilson, "Beyond Narrative: Imagination in the Sermon," *Listening to the Word: Studies in Honor of Fred B. Craddock*, ed. Gail R. O'Day and Thomas G. Long (Nashville: Abingdon Press, 1993), 131–46.

54. The search for new homiletic forms has begun: See Richard L. Eslinger, *A New Hearing* (Nashville: Abingdon Press, 1987); also John S. McClure, *The Four Codes of Preaching: Rhetorical Strategies* (Minneapolis: Fortress Press, 1991); and, recently, Eugene L. Lowry, "The Revolution in Sermon Shape," *Listening to the Word*, 93–112.

55. For a study of a changing rhetoric and Christian preaching, see George A. Kennedy, *Classical Rhetoric and Its Christian and Secular Tradition from Ancient to Modern Times* (Chapel Hill, N.C.: University of North Carolina Press, 1980). Because of Aristotelian commitments, Kennedy does not seem to do well with contemporary rhetoric. But see Sonja K. Foss, Karen A. Foss, and Robert Trapp, *Contemporary Perspectives on Rhetoric*, 2d ed. (Prospect Heights, Ill.: Waveland Press, 1985), for a survey with extensive bibliography.

56. For example, Norman L. Vos, *The Drama of Comedy* (Richmond: John Knox Press, 1966) and *For God's Sake Laugh* (Richmond: John Knox Press, 1967); and also, M. C. Hyers, ed., *Holy Laughter: Essays on Religion in the Comic Perspective* (New York: Seabury Press, 1969). See a sophisticated essay by Nathan A. Scott, Jr., "The Bias of Comedy and the Narrow Escape of Faith," *The Broken Center: Studies in the Theological Horizon of Modern Literature* (New Haven, Conn.: Yale University Press, 1966), 77-118.

57. Augustine's *On Christian Doctrine* is a work that deals with apologetic strategy, biblical interpretation and rhetoric; see Eugene TeSelle, *Augustine's Strategy as an Apologist* (Villanova, Pa.: Villanova University Press, 1974).

58. Hugh Blair, *Lectures on Rhetoric and Belles Letters*, 2 vols., ed. Harold F. Harding (Carbondale and Edwardsville, Ill.: Southern Illinois University Press, 1965); Richard Whately, *Elements of Rhetoric*, ed. Douglas Ehninger (Carbondale and Edwardsville, Ill.: Southern Illinois University Press, 1963). The full title of Whately's work was *Elements of Rhetoric, Comprising an Analysis of the Laws of Moral Evidence and of Persuasion, with Rules for Argumentative Composition and Elocution* [1828]. His work exerted tremendous influence over patterns of American homiletic thought into the twentieth century.

59. Frederick J. Hoffman, *The Mortal No: Death and the Modern Imagination* (Princeton, N.J.: Princeton University Press, 1964).

60. See Paul Elmen, *The Restoration of Meaning to Contemporary Life* (Garden City, N.Y.: Doubleday & Co., 1958), part II.

61. Wheelwright, *Metaphor and Reality*, 16, 33–38.

62. Arthur Herzog, *The B.S. Factor: The Theory and Technique of Faking It in America* (Baltimore: Penguin Books, 1974).

63. See Alexandre Vinet, *Homiletics* (New York: Ivison & Phinney, 1866), first published after Vinet's death in 1847. A remarkable work that influenced contemporary understandings of preaching, Vinet's *Homiletics* should be reissued. John A. Broadus, *A Treatise on the Preparation and Delivery of Sermons* (New York: A. C. Armstrong & Son, 1901) was first published in 1870. The book survives in abbreviated form as edited by Jesse Burton Weatherspoon: *On the Preparation and Delivery of Sermons* (New York: Harper & Brothers, 1944).

64. The death of God theology, circa 1960–65, featured works by Thomas J. J. Altizer, William Hamilton, Paul van Buren, Richard Rubenstein, and, from a Barthian perspective, Gabriel Vahanian. Though diverse, they rightly chronicled the "death" of cultural God-consciousness, an event which may have occurred in the 1950s. For an assessment, see Langdon Gilkey, *Naming the Whirlwind: The Renewal of God-Language* (New York: Bobbs-Merrill Co., 1969), 107–45.

65. For example, see Henry Moore's work in the Brooklyn Botanic Garden, *Museum without Walls: Henry Moore in New York City* (Camp Hill, Pa.: Book-of-the-Month Club, n.d.); for a survey of the same emphasis in literature, see Wylie Sypher, *Loss of the Self in Modern Literature and Art* (New York: Random House, 1962) and Julian N. Hartt, *The Lost Image of Man* (Baton Rouge, La.: Louisiana State University Press, 1963). Not surprisingly, Sypher and Hartt both wrote in the early 1960s and reviewed the previous decade.

66. Martin Esslin, *The Theatre of the Absurd* (Garden City, N.Y.: Doubleday & Co., 1961).

67. As does Goetz in Jean-Paul Sartre's Nietzschean drama, *The Devil and the Good Lord* (New York: Alfred A. Knopf, 1960), 140–43.

68. Yossarian, in Joseph Heller's, *Catch-22* (New York: Dell Publishing Co., 1962), rows off to Sweden rather than conform to society, symbolized by the army and a prospect of marriage.

69. *Zwischen der Zeiten* ("Between the Times," 1922–33), was a journal founded by Barth and Friedrich Gogarten.

70. Dwight Macdonald, "The String Untuned," *New Yorker* (March 10, 1962).

71. Criticism of technology is not new, for example, the works of Lewis Mumford from *Technics and Civilization* (1934) to *The Myth of the Machine: The Pentagon of Power* (1970). A Christian critique has been provided by Jacques Ellul, *The Technological Society*, trans. John Wilkinson (New York: Alfred A. Knopf, 1964), and more recently *The Technological System*, trans. Joachim Neugroschel (New York: Continuum, 1980).

72. See Ernest Becker, *The Denial of Death* (New York: Free Press, 1973).

73. Rieff, *The Triumph of the Therapeutic: Uses of Faith after Freud.*

74. Robert W. Jenson, *A Religion against Itself* (Richmond: John Knox Press, 1967).

75. Gustav Aulén, *Christus Victor: An Historical Study of the Three Main Types of the Idea of Atonement*, trans. A. G. Hebert (New York: Macmillan Co., 1951).

76. H. Richard Niebuhr, *Christ and Culture* (New York: Harper & Brothers, 1951).

77. Karl Barth, *Nein! Antwort an Emil Brunner* (Munich: C. Kaiser, 1934); for the English translation, see *Natural Theology*, trans. Peter Fraenkel (London: Centenary Press, 1946), 65–128.

78. On anti-Semitism in the Christian scriptures, see Rosemary Radford Ruether, *Faith and Fratricide: The Theological Roots of Anti-Semitism* (New York: Seabury Press, 1974). On sexism in Christian scriptures, among many works, see Elisabeth Schüssler Fiorenza, *Bread Not Stone.*

Chapter 4. Preaching and Method

1. Alan Bennett, Peter Cook, Jonathan Miller, and Dudley Moore, *Beyond the Fringe* (New York: Random House, 1963), 80. The skit was titled, "Take a Pew."

2. Is sermon form determined psychologically? One wonders because, for many preachers, sermon outlines may be compulsively the same no matter what text or topic is being preached. Are preachers expressing some sort of deep structure from within themselves? Could sermon design be diagnostic—depressive structures, obsessive–compulsive structures, schizoid structures, etc.? There is a sparse literature on the subject from the early work of Leslie J. Tizard, *Preaching: The Art of Communication* (New York: Oxford University Press, 1958) to the more recent work of Hans van der Geest, *Presence in the Pulpit*, trans. Douglas W. Stott (Atlanta: John Knox Press, 1981).

3. For discussion, see Emil L. Fackenheim, *Metaphysics and Historicity* (Milwaukee: Marquette University Press, 1961).

4. Here I am indebted to the thought of Paul Tillich. See his essay, "The World Situation," in *The Christian Answer*, 1–44.

5. For example, compare an ordered peasant interior by Dutch artist Jan Vermeer (1632–1675) with Marc Chagall's astonishing "I and the Village" (Museum of Modern Art, New York: Mrs. Simon Guggenheim Fund).

6. William Makepeace Thackeray, *Vanity Fair: A Novel without a Hero* (London: Bradbury & Evans, 1848).

7. William Faulkner, *The Sound and the Fury* (New York: Jonathan Cape and Harrison Smith, 1929). For discussion, Jean-Paul Sartre, "Time in Faulkner: *The Sound and the Fury*," *William Faulkner: Three Decades of Criticism*, ed. Frederick J. Hoffman and Olga W. Vickery (New York: Harcourt, Brace & World, 1960), 225–32.

8. Lawrence Durrell, *Justine* (1957); *Balthazar* (1958); *Mountolive* (1959); *Clea* (1960); all published in New York by E. P. Dutton Co., 1960.

9. For example, see Edoardo Sanguinetti, "Capriccio Italiano," trans. Raymond Rosenthal, *The Award Avant-Garde Reader*, ed. Gil Orlovitz (New York: Universal Publishing Award Books, 1965), 210–38. Notice that our usual syntax must be altered to represent simultaneity.

10. See Aron Gurwitsch, *The Field of Consciousness* (Pittsburgh: Duquesne University Press, 1964).

11. Owen Barfield, *Speaker's Meaning* (Middletown, Conn.: Wesleyan University Press, 1967), 42–49, suggests that the idea of gravity could not have been thought until word meanings changed to permit such thinking to occur.

12. George Steiner in *After Babel*, 79, writes, "Humboldt is one of the very short list of writers and thinkers on language—it would

include Plato, Vico, Coleridge, Saussure, Roman Jakobson—who have said anything that is new and comprehensive." Steiner provides a helpful survey of Humboldt's thought, pp. 79–88.

13. Whately, *Elements of Rhetoric* (1828).

14. For a critique of historical-critical method, see Walter Wink, *The Bible in Human Transformation: Toward a New Paradigm for Biblical Study* (Philadelphia: Fortress Press, 1975), chap. I. While Wink's critique is generally on target, his New Paradigm seems to be an old Jungian orientation.

15. Among many studies, see Daniel Patte, *What Is Structural Exegesis?* (Philadelphia: Fortress Press, 1976); Edgar V. McKnight, *Meaning in Texts: The Historical Shaping of a Narrative Hermeneutics* (Philadelphia: Fortress Press, 1978); See also John Sturrock, ed., *Structuralism and Since: From Lévi-Strauss to Derrida* (New York: Oxford University Press, 1979).

16. For a broad survey, see Edgar V. McKnight, *The Bible and the Reader: An Introduction to Literary Criticism* (Philadelphia: Fortress Press, 1985); for another, see Robert Detweiler, *Story, Sign, and Self: Phenomenology and Structuralism as Literary-Critical Methods* (Missoula, Mont.: Scholars Press, 1978). From the standpoint of contemporary literary theory, see Terry Eagleton, *Literary Theory: An Introduction* (Minneapolis: University of Minnesota Press, 1983).

17. For example, George A. Kennedy, *New Testament Interpretation through Rhetorical Criticism* (Chapel Hill, N.C.: University of North Carolina Press, 1984); see also Burton L. Mack, *Rhetoric and the New Testament* (Minneapolis: Fortress Press, 1990). We need a literature relating biblical criticism to more modern modes of rhetorical theory.

18. Wolfgang Iser, *The Implied Reader: Patterns of Communication in Prose Fiction from Bunyan to Beckett* (1975); and *The Act of Reading: A Theory of Aesthetic Response* (1978), both published by Johns Hopkins University Press. See also Jane P. Tompkins, ed., *Reader-Response Criticism from Formalism to Post-Structuralism* (Baltimore: Johns Hopkins University Press, 1980).

19. As examples, we cite the several works of Gerd Theissen, such as *Sociology of Early Palestinian Christianity* (Philadelphia: Fortress Press, 1978) and *Social Reality and the Early Christians* (Minneapolis: Fortress Press, 1992); see also John G. Gager, *Kingdom and Community: The Social World of Early Christianity* (Englewood Cliffs, N.J.: Prentice Hall, 1975).

20. A number of theologians seem to be going back to the nineteenth century, prior to the rise of neo-orthodoxy, to begin

again. For a sense of theology's unfinished tasks, see Peter C. Hodgson and Robert H. King, eds., *Christian Theology: An Introduction to Its Traditions and Tasks* (Philadelphia: Fortress Press, 1982), 1–27.

21. The single-verse text may have been developed by French court preachers after Louis XIV who were eager to demonstrate oratorical technique, but Brilioth reports a work in 1689 by J. B. Carpzov the Younger in which he offers one hundred different ways of preaching Psalm 14:7; see Yngve Brilioth, *A Brief History of Preaching* (Philadelphia: Fortress Press, 1965), 131.

22. My translation. For discussion of the passage, see my essay "Preaching and Interpretation," *Interpretation* 35, no. 1 (January 1981): 46–58.

23. The topics listed have been drawn from actual seminar discussion with different groups of ministers.

24. See the careful tracing of the method of distillation through rational hermeneutics by Hans W. Frei, *The Eclipse of Biblical Narrative: A Study of Eighteenth- and Nineteenth-Century Hermeneutics* (New Haven, Conn.: Yale University Press, 1974).

25. If you compare different commentaries offering a sentence summary of a text's subject matter, they are no more consistent than topics by preachers. The method of distillation is at fault; perhaps texts may have structural movement within definable fields of meaning, but passages do not contain a single "topic."

26. There are ten Luke commentaries on my shelf, and all of them fit the description!

27. In my *Homiletic*, 23–36, I have deliberately used the term "moves" rather than "points" to designate the several sections of a sermon.

28. See Amos Wilder, *The Language of the Gospel: Early Christian Rhetoric* (New York: Harper & Row, 1964), a book that turned biblical criticism toward literary form. With reference to homiletic theory, see Thomas G. Long, *Preaching and the Literary Forms of the Bible* (Philadelphia: Fortress Press, 1989).

29. Marshall McLuhan and Quentin Fiore, *The Medium Is the Message* (New York: Bantam Books, 1967); but see critical essays in Gerald Emanuel Stearn, ed., *McLuhan Hot and Cool* (New York: Dial Press, 1967), 191–263.

30. See my discussion in *Homiletic*, 293–301.

31. In Britain, the joke would feature an actress and a bishop; no doubt a tribute to the resiliency of the Anglican tradition!

32. Such variety need not be artificial. We human beings use

an astonishing repertoire of speech forms in day-to-day living. In preaching, we are doing public speaking, and such speaking should not be replaced by singing songs or role-playing. Nonetheless, forms of speech can affect our ways of speaking.

33. I have so argued with respect to sermon Introductions; see *Homiletic,* 90–91.

34. The term "point of view" is borrowed from literary criticism. The following studies will be helpful: Wayne C. Booth, *The Rhetoric of Fiction* (Chicago: University of Chicago Press, 1961); B. Uspensky, *A Poetics of Composition* (Berkeley, Calif.: University of California, 1973); and S. S. Lanser, *The Narrative Act* (Princeton, N.J.: Princeton University Press, 1981).

35. I have discussed point of view in preaching; see *Homiletic,* 55–68.

36. We suspect a reason that much preaching language does not form in consciousness and is not retained is because preachers are careless with point of view. Audiences are "triggery" with respect to perspectives. Thus, if an unaware preacher shifts point of view every two or three sentences, an audience, unfocused, will soon drift.

37. Literature on the demythologizing debate is extensive: Bultmann was criticized for imposing Heidegger's philosophical patterns on scripture, for being too much of a Lutheran with regard to scripture, for having a naive understanding of the modern scientific mentality, etc. The criticisms were no doubt true. Barth was criticized for demanding a "holy hermeneutic," for having no understanding of the hermeneutic issues, for separating scripture from the contemporary world, and for being too much of a Calvinist. Again most of the criticisms were probably true. Our position is simple: Something like demythologizing inevitably happens in the preparation of *every* sermon. For the debate, see Rudolf Bultmann and five critics, *Keryma and Myth: A Theological Debate,* ed. Hans Werner Bartsch (New York: Harper & Brothers, 1961), and Hans Werner Bartsch, ed., *Keryma and Myth: A Theological Debate,* Volume II, trans. Reginald H. Fuller (London: SPCK, 1962).

38. William James, *The Varieties of Religious Experience: A Study in Human Nature* (London: Longmans, Green & Co., 1902).

39. When the chapter on method was delivered as a lecture, the parable of the Rich Man and Lazarus was listed in the Anglican lectionary as a passage to be preached within forthcoming weeks. Though the passage seems structurally set and therefore may not

demonstrate rearrangements that are usual in the homiletic task, I retain the passage; it has other pedagogical virtues.

40. I have preached the parable only once and then with the addendum. What are the issues? Most parable scholars suppose that vv. 27–31 have been added to an original parable as a reference to the resurrection of Jesus Christ. The added verses may have had special reference to Jews who did not respond to news of the risen Christ. Obviously, the parable can be preached with or without the extra verses. Lectionaries are not law; so, in our example, we will omit vv. 27–31. For a summary discussion of the textual problems, see Bernard Brandon Scott, *Hear Then the Parable* (Minneapolis: Fortress Press, 1989), 142–46.

41. The so-called Jesus Seminar does not list Luke 16:19–31 as an authentic Jesus parable. According to their system of ranking, vv. 27–31 are *not* original Jesus material. But the group split with regard to vv. 19–26, some arguing that the sharp reversal is typical of Jesus, whereas others regard the passage as a product of Luke's polemic against wealth. See Robert W. Funk, Bernard Brandon Scott, and James R. Butts, *The Parables of Jesus: Red Letter Edition: A Report of the Jesus Seminar* (Sonoma, Calif.: Polebridge Press, 1988), 64.

42. For a summary discussion of the shift in parable study, see Norman Perrin, *Jesus and the Language of the Kingdom: Symbol and Metaphor in New Testament Interpretation* (Philadelphia: Fortress Press, 1976), 89–205. Recent parable interpretation seems to have developed in two phases: early works influenced by the "New Hermeneutic" were R. Funk, *Language, Hermeneutic, and Word of God* (1966); E. Linnemann, *Jesus of the Parables* (1966); D. Via, *The Parables* (1967); as well as books by John Dominic Crossan, *In Parables* (1973); *The Dark Interval* (1975); and *Raid on the Articulate* (1976). A second wave of studies was influenced by forms of literary criticism: J. Breech, *The Silence of Jesus* (1983); J. D. Crossan, *Finding Is the First Act* (1979) and *Cliffs for Fall* (1980); R. Funk, *Jesus as Precursor* (1975) and *Parables and Presence* (1982); M. A. Tolbert, *Perspectives on the Parables* (1979); B. B. Scott, *Jesus, Symbol-Maker for the Kingdom* (1981) and *Hear Then the Parable* (1989); J. R. Donahue, *The Gospel in Parable* (1988). During the same period, there were rather more traditional interpretations, drawing on historical-critical research, e.g., K. Bailey, *Poet and Peasant* (1976) and *Through Peasant Eyes* (1980). I have been much helped by the work of Bernard Brandon Scott, whose *Hear Then the Parable* (Philadelphia: Fortress Press,

1989) is a comprehensive commentary on all the parables. The book is especially useful for preachers.

43. Actually, "following along with the original narrative" is usual with parables, because parables achieve their effect by unfolding episode after episode. With other kinds of biblical material, a rearrangement of sequence is more *usual*.

44. Although one ancient Greek manuscript supplies the name *Neuēs;* see Joseph A. Fitzmyer, S.J., *The Gospel according to Luke (X–XXIV)* (Garden City, N.Y.: Doubleday & Co., 1985), 1130.

45. See references to purple and linen in Prov. 31:22 and Esth. 8:15.

46. Joachim Jeremias, *The Parables of Jesus,* trans. S. H. Hooke (New York: Charles Scribner's Sons, 1972), 184.

47. Wild dogs eat corpses of the cursed dead in 1 Kings 14:11; 16:4; 21:23–24; 22:38. For discussion, see B. B. Scott, *Hear Then the Parable,* 151.

48. See David L. Mealand, *Poverty and Expectation in the Gospels* (London: SPCK, 1980), chap. 3; see also Jacques Dupont, O.S.B., "The Poor and Poverty in the Gospels and Acts," in A. George et al., *Gospel Poverty: Essays in Biblical Theology,* trans. Michael D. Guinan, O.F.M. (Chicago: Franciscan Herald Press, 1977), 25–52; and Bruce J. Malina, "Wealth and Poverty in the New Testament and Its World," *Interpretation* 41, no. 4 (October 1987): 354–67. A more recent work, Justo González, *Faith and Wealth: A History of Early Christian Ideas on the Origin, Significance, and Use of Money* (San Francisco: Harper & Row, 1980) is helpful.

49. Scott, *Hear Then the Parable,* 159, citing Robert Frost's "Mending Wall," *The Complete Poems of Robert Frost* (New York: Henry Holt & Co., 1959), 47–48.

50. Early in the century, Hugo Gressmann collected an impressive number of Jewish and Egyptian rich man/poor man–in-heaven folktales; see *Vom reichen Mann und armen Lazarus* (Berlin: Verlag der Königl. Academie der Wissenschaften, 1918). Most books on the parables of Jesus cite Gressmann to establish the genre of the parable of the Rich Man and Lazarus.

51. For a devastating documentation of the increase of poverty in America, see Greg J. Duncan, "Economic Poverty—Causes and Effects," in Paul Plenge Parker, ed., *Standing with the Poor: Theological Reflections on Economic Reality* (Cleveland: Pilgrim Press, 1992), 3–28.

52. Brian Young, *The Villein's Bible: Stories in Romanesque Carving* (London: Barrie & Jenkins, 1990), 84.

53. I do not mean to imply that preaching is a natural form of

conversation; preaching is unnatural. Preachers who try to speak in a casual conversational manner, sounding "natural," are actually deforming the gospel. Think of trying to sound everyday-casual when you speak a life and death Word of God!

54. The title of a fine book by Fred B. Craddock, *Overhearing the Gospel* (Nashville: Abingdon Press, 1978).

55. Contemporary parable interpretation has repudiated the notion that parables have a single teaching, a notion put forth by Adolph Jülicher and, subsequently, in a somewhat different fashion by Joachim Jeremias; for discussion, see B. B. Scott, *Hear Then the Parable*, 42–62.

56. Bertolt Brecht called his dramas "Parables for the Theater." He argued against the idea of catharsis, insisting that catharsis was the enemy of revolutionary change—people feel inwardly, but outwardly remain unchanged in their social allegiances. Therefore, in his dramas, he deliberately destroyed identifications that could lead to catharsis. Parables, he argued, by a kind of distancing, force people to see and act. Preachers often assume that feeling is a source of converting change, but suppose Brecht is right. For Brechtian theory, see *Brecht on Theatre: The Development of an Aesthetic*, trans. John Willett (New York: Hill & Wang, 1966).

Afterword: Looking toward a Future

1. An album by Bob Dylan titled "The Times They Are a-Changin'" was issued by Columbia Records in January 1964. The title song included stanzas addressed to "writers and critics," "mothers and fathers," as well as "senators, congressman;" all saying, in effect, the world is changing radically, so we must change as well.

2. For discussion, see David Halberstam, *The Next Century* (New York: William Morrow & Co., 1991), 55–78; also see Gerald Segal, *The World Affairs Companion: The Essential One-Volume Guide to Global Issues* (New York: Simon & Schuster, 1991), 1–13.

3. See *The Church and Transnational Corporations*, ed. Dean H. Lewis, *Church & Society* 74, no. 4 (March/April 1984).

4. See *Population Bulletin* 47, no. 4 (December 1992): 9; *American Demographics* 15, no. 2 (February 1993): 9–10.

5. Bloom, *The American Religion*, 266–71.

6. See Justo and Catherine González, *The Liberated Pulpit*

(Nashville: Abingdon Press, 1994), a book that deals with preaching as redefined by liberation movements.

7. See a helpful book by Peter C. Hodgson, *Revisioning the Church: Ecclesial Freedom in the New Paradigm* (Philadelphia: Fortress Press, 1988).

8. See Langdon Gilkey, "Plurality: Our New Situation," in *The Pastor as Servant,* ed. Earl E Shelp and Ronald H. Sunderland (New York: Pilgrim Press, 1986), 102–22.

9. Karl Barth, *Church Dogmatics,* I/2, 280–325.

10. The first task may involve preliminary theological considerations; see Paul F. Knitter, *No Other Name? A Critical Survey of Christian Attitudes toward the World Religions* (Maryknoll, N.Y.: Orbis Books, 1985); also, Owen C. Thomas, ed., *Attitudes toward Other Religions: Some Christian Interpretations* (Lanham, Md.: University Press of America, 1986).

11. The famous trials in which Presbyterian scholars Charles Augustus Briggs and Henry Preserved Smith were dismissed from the church were held in the 1890s. The *Auburn Affirmation* was signed in 1924. In between, there was continuous controversy.

12. I have discussed Fosdick and Barth in an article, "Preaching in an *Un*brave New World," *The Spire* (Summer/Fall 1988).

13. A line from Harry Emerson Fosdick, "What Is the Matter with Preaching?," *Harper's Magazine* 157 (July 1928). The article may also be found in Lionel Crocker, ed., *Harry Emerson Fosdick's Art of Preaching: An Anthology* (Springfield, Ill.: Charles C. Thomas, 1971), chap. 2.

14. Crocker, *Harry Emerson Fosdick's Art of Preaching,* 31.

15. Harry Emerson Fosdick, "Personal Counseling and Preaching," *Pastoral Psychology* 3, no. 22 (March 1952). Reprinted in Crocker, *Harry Emerson Fosdick's Art of Preaching,* chap. 5.

16. Barth, *The Preaching of the Gospel,* 42–43.

17. Elsewhere I have argued that black preaching did not succumb to personal therapeutic because it addressed the consciousness of a *people,* people who suffered racism in common. Likewise, black preachers did not tumble into biblicism, because they received scripture as a story of liberation with an eschatological horizon. See "Preaching, Hermeneutics, and Liberation," in P. P. Parker, ed., *Standing with the Poor,* 95–107.

18. Keith D. Miller, *Voice of Deliverance: The Language of Martin Luther King, Jr. and Its Sources* (New York: Macmillan Co., 1992), cites King's tendency to draw on material from other preachers, a

fairly normal activity in the 1950s, when books of sermons echoed in many pulpits. But King was an able rhetorician in his own right with a wide, wonderful social vision that exceeded his sources. For a splendid study of King's life and work, see Louis V. Baldwin's two volumes, *There Is a Balm in Gilead: The Cultural Roots of Martin Luther King, Jr.* (1990) and *To Make the Wounded Whole: The Cultural Legacy of Martin Luther King, Jr.* (1992), both published by Fortress Press.

19. Doug Marlette is author of the comic strip. For a sample, see *Kudzu* (New York: Ballantine Books, 1982).

20. J.N.D. Kelly, *Early Christian Doctrines* (New York: Harper & Row, 1960), 263–69.

21. See José Miranda, *Marx and the Bible: A Critique of the Philosophy of Oppression,* trans. John Eagleson (Maryknoll, N.Y.: Orbis Books, 1974).

22. See my *Preaching Jesus Christ,* chap. 4.

23. This is the title of a book by Matthew L. Lamb, *Solidarity with Victims: Toward a Theology for Social Transformation* (New York: Crossroad, 1982). The first two sentences of the book are, *"Vox victimarum vox Dei*—the cries of victims are the voice of God. The scandal of the Cross is the scandal of God identified with all the victims of history in the passion of Christ."

24. See Walter Wink, *Engaging the Powers: Discernment and Resistance in a World of Domination* (Minneapolis: Fortress Press, 1992). Previously, Wink has published *Naming the Powers* (Fortress, 1984) and *Unmasking the Powers* (Fortress, 1986).

25. Ross MacDonald, *The Doomsters* (New York: Bantam Books, 1958), 168.

26. For a helpful study of contemporary televangelism, see Carol Flake, *Redemptorama: Culture, Politics, and the New Evangelicalism* (New York: Penguin Books, 1988).

27. R. Bultmann, "Is Exegesis without Presuppositions Possible?" *Existence and Faith: Shorter Writings of Rudolf Bultmann* (New York: Meridian Books, 1960), 289–96; for interpretation, see Schubert M. Ogden, *Christ without Myth: A Study Based on the Theology of Rudolf Bultmann* (New York: Harper & Row, 1961), 44–64.

28. For a concise approach to the thought of Ricoeur, see Paul Ricoeur, "Philosophical Hermeneutics and Theological Hermeneutics: Ideology, Utopia, and Faith," *Studies in Religion/Sciences Religieuses* 5, no. 1 (University of Toronto Press, 1975): 14–33.

29. See Edward Farley, "Interpreting Situations: An Inquiry into the Nature of Practical Theology," in Lewis S. Mudge and

James N. Poling, eds., *Formation and Reflection: The Promise of Practical Theology* (Philadelphia: Fortress Press, 1987), 1–26. The article provides helpful bibliographical notes.

30. See Jenny Nelson, "Eyes out of Your Head: On Television Experience," *Critical Studies in Mass Communication* 6, no. 4 (December 1989): 387–403. Nelson labels TV watching as a "prereflective passive activity."

31. For a helpful guide to world theologies, see Justo L. González, *Out of Every Tribe and Nation: Christian Theology at the Ethnic Roundtable* (Nashville: Abingdon Press, 1992).

Index